Rev.
ERNest
Hodge

THE FORCE of STAR WARS

THE FORCE of STAR WARS

by Frank Allnutt

Published by

Bible Voice, Inc.   P.O. Box 7491

Van Nuys, California 91409

The author and publisher express appreciation to Charles Lippincott and to Twentieth Century-Fox for supplying information and photographs for this book.

To my loved ones,

Ruth

Garrett

Teddy

Lara

CONTENTS

PREFACE

The taxi rambled through Kansas City's inner city, and on into the suburbs, taking me to an unfamiliar destination. I was in town a day early and the day was to be filled with many opportunities to see old friends and make new ones—not to mention there were a few preconvention programs lined up to get delegates in the right frame of mind for the week-long events ahead.

But for some uncanny reason unknown to me then, I was being drawn to the outskirts of Kansas City by some irresistible force. Where was I headed? Why was I going?

My destination proved to be in a colorful shopping center, in a plush new suburb south of town.

As the taxi pulled away from the curb leaving me behind, I stood on the sidewalk, looking up at the giant marquee of a glittering new movie theater, and read:

Long ago, in a galaxy far, far away,
there were. . .
STAR WARS

It was a little past noon on this bright, hot Sunday. Though the box office wouldn't open for another hour and a half, a line already was beginning to form.

Why was I standing there, sweltering in a suit and tie, waiting to see this film called *Star Wars?*

More and more people came to swell the waiting line around me. The growing crowd seemed charged with an unusual air of expectation. I, too, began to feel a tinge of excited anticipation—but why, I didn't know. Actually, I had only heard about *Star Wars* and never so much as read a single review on it.

I sensed at that point I was destined for some special reason to see *Star Wars* this day, but I couldn't for the life of me figure out why!

After waiting for what amounted to nearly two and a half hours, I was seated and the house lights finally went down. Suddenly the spectacle of *Star Wars* burst upon the giant screen.

What happened in the next two hours had a mesmerizing effect not only on me but on the entire audience that had packed the theater and spanned the age spectrum from toddlers to senior citizens.

As a motion picture, *Star Wars* was a

thorough triumph. Among many other things, it reminded me of *Mary Poppins* and other fantasy films I worked on during my early days in publicity at the Walt Disney studio. Walt would have loved *Star Wars!*

I don't remember much about the taxi ride back to my hotel. The scenery rushed by in a blur as thoughts churned and churned. Later that evening, a distillation of ideas from my mind began to spill out the incredibly complex mixture of notions that had been sloshing around in my head since seeing the film—notions about the film itself, from books I had written and others I had read, the world situation, and a fascination with the destiny of the world.

Scribbling these bits of thought down on paper as rapidly as possible, I witnessed in a short time the emergence of a rough outline for this book. I began to understand the reasons for *Star Wars'* tremendous impact on the senses of people as they viewed the spectacle in theaters across the country. Some of those reasons were obvious, and others less detectable, lying somewhere just beneath the surface of the film.

So I probed and probed my mind and began to see the depth of eternal truths in *Star Wars*—truths that could only be hinted at in a motion picture designed primarily to entertain. But the true essence of *Star Wars* goes far beyond the entertainment level, to touch upon such profound truths as where did the world come from and where is it going? Is there purpose in life? Is history hurtling ahead, uncontrollably into an unknown future, or is there some grand design that is unfolding before our very eyes? Is man capable of determining his own destiny, or is there a divine power, a *True Force*, that man can draw upon for purpose and guidance?

The result of my strange mission in Kansas City is this book. It explains the meanings behind the fascinating prophetic parables found in *Star Wars.*

Through reading this book, you will discover there *is* a True Force who created and controls the universe. What's more, you'll find that this Force is a personality who, as incredible as it may seem, loves you and has a wonderful plan for your life!

You are now embarking on an adventure that can help change your life for the better.

May the True Force be with you!

Frank Allnutt

Lake Arrowhead, California

Chapter 1

The Secret of
Star Wars' Popularity

At a theater in San Francisco, 1,500 people stood in line for three and a half hours to see *Star Wars,* but the theater could seat only 800. Up and down the long waiting line, scalpers were getting four times the face value of tickets.

In another part of the country, theaters were taking reservations for seeing *Star Wars* two days in advance.

Reports are that the film, which cost more than nine million dollars to make, broke even after its first week in release.

Motion picture trade magazines predicted that *Star Wars* will become the all-time, top-grossing picture in box-office history, beating out such blockbusters as *Jaws, The Godfather, Gone with the Wind* and *The Sound of Music.*

What makes *Star Wars* such a phenomenally popular motion picture? What is the secret behind its unprecedented success? What's it about? And who is the driving force behind it?

The New Hollywood

George Lucas, who wrote and directed *Star Wars*, belongs to a whole new generation of talented filmmakers in Hollywood. His first professional feature motion picture was *THX-1138*, which was an expanded version of the prize-winning film he produced while a cinematography student at the University of Southern California.

Then, in 1973, Lucas directed and co-wrote the enormously successful and critically acclaimed *American Graffiti.* This film has been hailed as *the* movie about American teenage life and rituals in the post-World War II years.

The crowning achievement, however, in the short, fantastically successful career of George Lucas has been *Star Wars.*

The Script Nobody Wanted

The idea for a space fantasy began to germinate in the fertile mind of George Lucas as early as 1971. A few years and some four total rewrites of the script later, he was ready to take his idea to Hollywood. But studio after studio turned the script down! At a time when Hollywood was churning out vulgarity, gore and sex, an idea like *Star Wars* just didn't seem to have the necessary elements for box-office success.

For example, it contained no profanity beyond an occasional "hell" or the like. There's no flinching violence. And there's not a single sex scene!

But Twentieth Century-Fox took a gamble and agreed to produce the film.

Good, Clean Adventure

Star Wars was designed by Lucas to be a good, clean adventure film for the entire family. In the studio's press kit, the canned "review" of *Star Wars* begins with this quotation:

> I have wrought my simple plan
> If I give some hour of joy
> To the boy who's half a man,
> Or the man who's half a boy.
> —Arthur Conan Doyle's
> preface to *The Lost World*

And the studio has a point. What boy who's half a man, or what man who's half a boy, never dreamed about blasting off into space to uncharted corners of the universe? Or what girl who's half a woman, or what woman who's half a girl, never dreamed about being a beautiful princess who is rescued from the evil warlord by a dashing prince charming?

Well, *Star Wars* was made for these kinds of people. It's a razzle-dazzle family movie, just as George Lucas conceived it to be. He has created an imaginative entertainment experience that is transporting audiences out of the theater and into an unknown galaxy, thousands of light-years from earth.

To Lucas, the motion picture medium is the most magnificent toy ever invented, and which he so adroitly manipulates to express his own fantasies, project his own nightmares and dreams, and to indulge in his own whimsies and secret desires. And the audiences love every minute of it!

Star Wars uses practically every technical wizardry known to modern film-making (plus a few specially invented ones, for good measure) to blend the not so polished hardware of modern space adventure with the romantic fantasies of sword and sorcery.

Fun and Fantasy

"It's fun—that's the word for this

movie," described Lucas. "Young people today don't have a fantasy life anymore; not the way we did. All they've got is *Kojak* and *Dirty Harry*. There are all these kids running around wanting to be killer cops. All the films they see are movies of disasters and insecurity and realistic violence."

Star Wars grew out of George Lucas' love affair with the *Flash Gordon* serials that were produced in the generation before him. But young George Lucas caught up with them on television reruns. Through these serials, plus books and comic books, he became a great fan of science fiction and space fantasy.

"I've always loved things like *Camelot* and *Treasure Island*," Lucas explained. "I've always loved adventure movies. Since the westerns died, there hasn't been any mythological fantasy realm available to young people, which is what I grew up on."

He went on to tell how he wanted to make an action movie—one in outer space like *Flash Gordon* used to be—ray guns, running around in spaceships, shooting at each other.

"I knew I wanted to have a big battle in outer space, a sort of dogfight thing," he said. "I wanted to make a movie about an old man and a kid. And I knew I wanted the old man to be a real old man and have a sort of teacher-student relationship with the kid. I wanted the old man to also be like a warrior. I wanted a princess, too, but I didn't want her to be a passive damsel in distress."

And so it came to pass that George Lucas, inspired by the likes of *Flash Gordon, The Wizard of Oz,* and other classics, accomplished in a grand way the things he had set out to do. For *Star Wars* has succeeded as a space fantasy that has been just as enthusiastically received by non-science fiction aficionados as by hard-core sci-fi freaks. The galactic world of *Star Wars* is one that people on this earth have never been to, but it's a world they may have encountered when years ago they dreamed about running away and having adventures that no one else had ever had.

The Great Galactic Adventure

Star Wars is a romantic tale about a young naive boy and a beautiful, spirited princess. It is an odyssey from farm-boy innocency to battlefield maturity and knowledge. It revives the concept of respecting the wisdom and place of elders, and reenacts the timeless cycle of passing the sword from one generation to the next. And it all happens in a world that existed far away and long ago, where the impossible is possible, and love and goodness triumph over evil.

The story follows the adventures of young Luke Skywalker (does the similar sounding names of "Luke" and "Lucas" suggest that Luke Skywalker is really George Lucas in disguise?). Luke is played by actor Mark Hamill, in his motion picture debut.

We follow Luke through exotic worlds uniquely different from our own, beginning at the small arid planet of Tatooine. From there, on the dusty Tatooine farm of his uncle Owen (Phil Brown) and his aunt Beru Lars (Shelagh Fraser), Luke plunges into an extraordinary intergalactic search for the kidnapped rebel, Princess Leia Organa (Carrie Fisher), from the planet Alderaan.

Luke is guided into this daring mission by Ben "Obi-wan" Kenobi (Alec Guinness), the last of the Jedi Knights, who were the guardians of peace and justice in the old days before the "dark times" came to the galaxy.

In a sleazy cabaret, a hangout for a nightmarish assortment of outlaw space creatures, Luke and Kenobi hire the dashing but cynical Han Solo (Harrison Ford) to pilot them through space aboard his Corellian pirate starship, the *Millennium Falcon.*

With Solo comes an unlikely copilot named Chewbacca (Peter Mayhew). "Chew" is a Wookie—a race of tall anthropoids with monkey-like faces, bodies covered with long hair, and large blue eyes. In some ways, Chew resembles the lion in *The Wizard of Oz.* But then, too, he looks like he might have come from *The Planet of the Apes.*

In the beginning of the story, we meet the robots, See-Threepio (C-3PO) and Artoo-Detoo (R2-D2). Threepio is a gold-plated humanoid that very much resembles a luxury version of the Tin Man from *The Wizard of Oz.* Artoo, on the other hand, is an innocent, childlike robot that resembles a globe-topped trash receptacle on wheels. Threepio speaks in an undisguised and quite proper British accent, while Artoo communicates audibly through a series of bleeps, whirs and whines. These two are the Laurel and Hardy of the new age of science fiction films, for sure!

Threepio is played by British actor Anthony Daniels, and Artoo is played by fellow countryman, Kenny Baker, who stands three feet, eight inches tall.

This incredible assortment of misfits ultimately make battle with Grand Moff Tarkin (Peter Cushing), the wicked Governor of the Imperial Outland regions, and with Darth Vader (David Prowse), the malevolent Dark Lord of the Sith, who uses supernatural powers to aid Governor Tarkin in the destruction of the rebellion against the oppressive Galactic Empire.

In the space battle of Yavin, Luke hurls with dizzying speed into a terrifying climactic space battle over the huge man-made planet destroyer called the Death Star.

But the real hero of *Star Wars* is the unseen supernatural power that created and binds together the universe—the Force. In the final analysis, *Star Wars* is a classic tale of the people of the Force (the good guys), led by Luke and Kenobi, his mentor, against the bad guys—the occultic Darth Vader and the evil rulers of the Galactic Empire.

Why Is Star Wars So Popular?

The question is an interesting one, because the fascination of *Star Wars* lies beneath its obvious surface of good, clean entertainment for the entire family.

Darth Vader is one good reason for the film's popularity. Darth is the personification of all that is evil. No excuses are given for his evil nature, no rationalizations. It can't be blamed on his relationship with his father, nor has his environment fostered hostile, aggressive tendencies. Darth is evil because he wants to be, and for this reason the audiences can boo and hiss him for what he is. He is the arch-villain and therefore *deserves* to incur the wrath of the audiences.

Just as evil is clearly depicted in *Star Wars,* so is goodness! This is the first movie in a long while where the good guys win, and everybody who is a good guy lives happily ever after, or until the sequel to *Star Wars* is made, that is.

The Search for Reality

George Lucas, because he wrote and directed *Star Wars,* probably knows more about his film than anyone. But I wonder if, as he says, people really like the film because it allows them to live out childhood fantasies. Perhaps the opposite is true. Perhaps the youth of today, especially, see the world they are living in as artificial, a fantasy, if you will, and really want to find reality. *Star Wars* gives them a glimpse of reality—a hope for something more meaningful than the fantasy of everyday life so many people are living.

Now let me explain this. The world we live in is filled with fantasies just waiting for people to act them out. For example, the idea that the accumulation of things, and especially money, can bring true and lasting happiness is sheer fantasy. The playboy philosophy that a sex-centered life-style can bring true and lasting happiness is a deceptive fantasy, too. Does dope bring real happiness to a person's life? Or alcohol? You can make your own list. . . .

I believe the young people of today are becoming wise to these deceptions. They've seen too many frustrated if not ruined lives of people who searched in the wrong places for reality.

The values and morals of today are fabricating a fantasy society in America—an escape from reality. But young people of today want to find reality, and they're looking everywhere to find it. *Star Wars* is a fantasy with a message about reality. It says to the viewer, "Listen! There's something better in life than wallowing in the mud of pornography, dope, materialism and vain philosophies. You have a higher calling—a calling to be somebody, to do something. You have a date with destiny. You have potential in you that you haven't begun to develop. There is a Force in the universe that you need to be plugged into. It's a power that is the source of goodness and justice. It's a power that can take a failure of a person and make him a success, a miserable person and make him joyful, and a wasted person and give him purpose."

That's what *Star Wars* is saying to the people of America, and that's why they are seeing it, and some of them again and again.

Star Wars is a prophetic parable which, as the remainder of this book will explain, can change your life for the better! You, too, can know and experience the real secret behind the irresistible attraction of *Star Wars*.

STAR WARS

Released by 20th Century-Fox

Luke Skywalker (**Mark Hamill**) covers his escape to the Corellian pirate starship.

Chapter 2

The Rise and Fall of the Republic

In a galaxy long ago and far, far away, according to legend, there was the Republic. Its origins and location among the millions of stars in the universe had been lost in the endless retelling of the legend, much like the legend of the lost city of Atlantis. What mattered, really, was to know that the Republic had existed.

The people of the Republic, so the story goes, worshiped a deity called the Force. Said to have created the entire universe and all that is within it, the Force was also the source of supernatural power for the believers of the Republic. Consequently, the Republic grew to become the most powerful of all the empires in the universe.

From the very beginning the Republic was a thriving system. It was blessed with noble men of far-reaching vision who colonized the planets of star system after star system.

Hardy men and women pioneered these colonies, many times in the face of never-before-heard-of dangers and hardships.

Trade was established among the insectoids, reptilians and anthropoids of even the most distant systems, and trade and commerce thrived throughout the universe.

The governmental structure of the Republic was a model for the other systems of the universe to follow. Every occupied planet in the Republic's sphere of influence was represented in the Senate. It was under this wise body of good and just rulers, and the protection of the Jedi Knights, of course, that the Republic throve and grew.

The small star systems welcomed the Republic as a faithful military and trade ally, for there was never a system—nor has there been one since—that boasted the military might of the Jedi Knights. Endowed with supernatural powers from the Force, these highly respected Jedis manned the vast fleet of heavily armed and otherwise vastly superior starcruisers. Under the protection of the Jedi Knights, the boundaries of the Republic expanded in leapfrog fashion from star system to star system.

Just as the knights of King Arthur's Round Table worshiped Almighty God, the Jedis followed the ways of the Force. To them, the protection of the galactic system was a sacred trust.

Corruption from Within

No one is certain exactly how or when it began, but, in time, the people of the Republic slowly drifted away from following the ways of the Force. Instead, they looked to the Senate for the answers to life's problems. Affluence gave way to materialism, and the wealth and power that once was used to develop new star systems were being concentrated more and more on personal luxuries and comforts at home. Among businessmen honest gain was scoffed at in favor of get-rich schemes and . . . yes, out-and-out piracy and other criminal dealings became commonplace. The once admirable goals of the Republic, based on the ways of the Force, had slowly been replaced by self-centered ones and a shameful deterioration of moral values.

As usually happens at this point in the life of any society, there appeared evil people whose blind greed drove them into gaining control of the Senate's power and the Republic's official wealth. This marked the beginning of the decline of the Old Republic. Personal freedoms began to disappear, and only the most devout and most daring continued to practice the ways of the Force, and then not openly.

The Rise and Fall of Nations

What had happened to the legendary Republic of *Star Wars* has been observed over and over again in other nations in the history of the world: Morality declines, the family unit is fractured, atheism creeps in and individual liberties are taken away by totalitarian governments.

We can see in the history of nations that there is an apparent pattern to the rise and fall of the world's empires. The very wise and very observant Plato wrote generations ago of another Republic:

"The citizens . . . chafe impatiently at the least touch of authority, and at length . . . they cease to care even for the laws, written or unwritten . . . and this is the fair and glorious beginning out of which springs tyranny. . . . The excessive increase of anything often causes a reaction in the opposite direction. . . . Tyranny naturally arises out of democracy, and the most aggravated form of tyranny and slavery out of the most extreme form of liberty."

The story of the Old Republic in *Star Wars* has many counterparts in history. One of the most notable is the nation of Israel. To begin with, they are alike in their religious character. The people of the Old Republic worshiped the Force, and the people of Israel worshiped the God of the Bible. It was through the people of the Old Republic that goodness and justice, centered in the ways of the Force, would be carried throughout the universe. And, it was through the people of Israel that the Bible was to be recorded and preserved and taught to the people of the world.

But the people of the Old Republic turned their backs on the Force. All but a few of them, anyway. Still, there rose from the dust of Tatooine the person of Obi-wan Kenobi, who led his people to salvation in the face of their enemies. In like manner, out of the people of Israel there would rise the Messiah—God in the form of a man— who would be the Savior of His people. When the Messiah—Jesus Christ—did come, many Israelites, out of spiritual blindness, turned their backs on Him. But a few believed and followed Him, joined in their ranks by a growing number of non-Jews.

The people of the Republic were given the universe to develop and rule. In similar fashion, God gave the children of Israel their own land which would be theirs forever, the land of Palestine. Now, there is good reason for this. In order to carry out the teaching of God's Word from the Holy Scriptures, and in order to be present at the time of the coming of the Messiah, the people of Israel would have to have identity as a people: They would need their own nation.

But like the people of the Republic, the children of Israel suffered the consequences to their nation for turning away from God.

Led Out of Bondage

The book of Exodus tells us how the Israelites, who because of their sin were allowed by God to be taken captive into Egypt, were led out of bondage by Moses. But they soon forgot what God had done for them and returned to worshiping false gods. God punished them by causing them to wander in the wilderness for many years. But, at last, He permitted them to cross into the land He had promised them through their patriarch, Abraham.

The modern nation of Israel today occupies some of this land, which is a matter of great concern and debate among the nations of the world.

The twelve tribes of Israel succeeded in forming a single government, ruled by a king, around 1000 B.C. Later, the nation split into two segments. The ten northern tribes retained the name Israel, and the two southern tribes took upon themselves the name Judea.

In time, the chosen people of God again sinned terribly as a people. They began ignoring God's laws, their morals declined, and they returned to worshiping the heathen idols. God punished them by allowing the Assyrians in 721 B.C. to invade and conquer Israel (the ten northern tribes) and carry them off into captivity.

A few generations later, in 605 B.C., Nebuchadnezzar, king of Babylon, overran the two tribes of Judea in the south, destroyed the city of Jerusalem and its Temple of God, and eventually took the Judeans back to Babylon where they remained in bondage for seventy years.

The book of Ezra carries the account of how the chosen people of God, after the dispersion by the Assyrians and the Babylonians, returned to the promised land, where they eventually rebuilt the Temple in Jerusalem.

By A.D. 70, the Jews, because of their spiritual blindness, had permitted their own

Messiah to be killed, had made a sham of Temple worship, and were drifting farther and farther from following the ways of God. So God once more permitted their enemies to destroy their cities and scatter the people throughout the world. This was accomplished when the Roman Titus and his legions invaded the Holy Land, leveled Jerusalem and tore down the magnificent Temple, stone by stone, seeking out the melted gold gilding.

Return of the Remnant

Throughout the centuries that followed the Roman dispersion, the children of Israel maintained their identity. Even the Nazi holocaust of World War II could not destroy the Jews as a people! Why have the Jews survived under such great odds? Because God is faithful to His promises, even if His people are not faithful to Him.

The Jews never gave up hope of returning to their promised land. God had promised that He would restore them to it in the "latter days":

"Thus says the Lord God, 'Behold, I will take the sons of Israel from among the nations where they have gone, and I will gather them from every side and bring them into their own land; and I will make them one nation in the land, on the mountains of Israel; and one king will be king for all of them; and they will no longer be two nations, and they will no longer be divided into two kingdoms" (Ezekiel 37:21,22, *NASB*).

This amazing prophecy saw the beginning of its fulfillment on May 14, 1948, when the new nation of Israel was reborn in the land of Palestine. The children of Israel had returned to their land for the third time, and perhaps the last time. God has done in our lifetime what He said He would do hundreds and hundreds of years ago!

Through the power of the Force, the people of the Old Republic, after many years, were on the road to reviving the glory which was once theirs. And, now, through the grace of God, the people of Israel are back in their land, restored as a chosen people of God. Though the Israelites, as a nation, continue to suffer spiritual blindness in that they refuse to recognize that Jesus Christ is their Messiah, the Bible promises that their blindness will be removed at the end of the age and they will be saved as a nation:

"Israel has experienced a hardening in part until the full number of the Gentiles has come in. And so all Israel will be saved, as it is written: 'The Deliverer will come from Zion; he will turn godlessness away from Jacob. And this is my covenant with them when I take away their sins'" (Romans 11:25-27).

The Tragedy of Babylon

There is also a *future* nation mentioned in the Bible that will have many similarities with the Old Republic. Earlier, we mentioned the ancient empire of Babylon, which was ruled over by King Nebuchadnezzar. Babylon was a nation of idol worshipers. In fact, Nebuchadnezzar even had a gigantic statue of himself built for his subjects to worship! Babylon was so wicked that even today the term Babylon is used to describe any sinful city or nation.

It is interesting that there are many prophecies about Babylon in the Bible which have no historical fulfillment. This has led many Bible scholars to believe that these prophecies pertain to a still future empire that is so wicked that it is called "Babylon the Great" in the book of Revelation. It is believed that this future Babylon will turn out to be the most powerful, wealthiest, and most blessed nation of all time.

From such lengthy passages in the Bible as Jeremiah 50 and 51, and Revelation 17 and 18, as well as many others, we can learn much about this future Babylon the Great.

The Bible tells us it will be a nation blessed by God above all other nations. It will have land, great natural resources in abundance, and much, much wealth. In fact, it will be the commercial and industrial center of the world. The reasons for this are interesting. God will give all these blessings to the people of Babylon to enable them to help develop other nations of the world and especially to teach other nations about Himself and His Son, Jesus Christ. But just like the people of Israel and the people of the Old Republic, the Babylonians will turn from worshiping God. Worst of all, they will turn to worship Satan!

The Babylonians will no longer use their wealth for God's purposes, but, instead to feed their own insatiable materialistic appetites. And what will God do? You guessed it! Just as the people of the Old Republic lost their empire when they turned from the ways of the Force, and just as God allowed the children of Israel to be driven from their land—and all other nations who turned from Him to lose their blessings as a nation—He will destroy Babylon the Great and everyone in it. Of course, as always has been the case in every other nation destroyed by God, there will be a small number of people who will have been faithful to God to the end and will be saved.

Are We Next?

What about the United States? Are we next in line to fall under God's judgment? Our country was founded upon Christian principles, yet only a small percentage of Americans can claim to be children of God in the sense that they believe in Jesus Christ as their Lord and Savior and follow His teachings. Sadly, a great number of our fellow Americans have turned their backs on God to follow a self-destructive course of trying to live their lives without Him.

There are many modern thinkers who believe the United States is headed for serious trouble. They see alarming trends not only in the country's spiritual life, but also in its morals, its regard for the law, economics and world involvement. These trends, they believe, could bring about the same kind of decadence from within that brought about the fall of Rome and perhaps every other major power in history.

Some of the West's best-known statesmen and a number of distinguished scholars, including former Secretary of State Dean Rusk and former British Prime Minister Lord Hume, descended upon the Center for Study of the American Experience at the University of Southern California in March 1977 for a conference called "The Future of the West."

In one of the sessions, French author and scholar Jean Gimpel asked, "Is the cycle which has been observed previously in other civilizations and cultures—that of ascension, followed by stability and dominance, concluding with disruption and decline—inevitable for the current society in governing structures of the West?" Then he answered his own question: "It is inevitable." And the majority of the delegates to the conference agreed.

Alexander Solzhenitsyn, outstanding Pulitzer Prize-winning Russian author, warned of the growing Soviet military superiority in the March 15, 1976 issue of the *U.S. News and World Report:* "I wouldn't be surprised at the sudden and imminent fall of the West. . . . The West is on the verge of a collapse created by its own hands."

British intellectual Malcolm Muggeridge, who is an authority on worldwide communism, has been quoted to say that, in his opinion, we are already in the second Dark Age!

How Should We Then Live?

Francis A. Schaeffer, theologian and philosopher and one of the leading evangelical thinker of our day, writes in *How Should We Then Live?*: "Overwhelming pressures . . . are progressively preparing modern people to accept a manipulative, authoritarian government. Unhappily, many of these pressures are upon us now."

He defined these pressures as: economic breakdown; war or the serious threat of war; the chaos of violence, especially random or political violence and indiscriminate terrorism, in an individual nation or in the world; the radical redistribution of the wealth of the world; a growing shortage of food and other natural resources in the world.

There are only two alternatives, Dr. Schaeffer reminds us: "First, imposed order or, second, our society once again affirming that base which gave freedom without chaos in the first place—God's revelation in the Bible and His revelation through Christ."

What in the World Is Happening?

Anyone who reads the daily newspapers, or listens to radio or watches TV, knows that serious problems face the future of the nation and the world. Is there a moral for us in the lost Republic of *Star Wars?* Will we learn the lessons of history? Or will history repeat itself and will we see America continue its decline? Will we in our generation see the last great bastion of liberty on earth toppled from within?

The alternative, as Dr. Schaeffer suggests, is to turn to the base that gave us freedom in the first place: God's revelation in the Bible and His revelation through Jesus Christ.

George Lucas so vividly, but perhaps unknowingly, pointed to this essential truth in *Star Wars.* It was only when the rebel Alliance turned to following the ways of the Force that they were able to overcome the oppression of the evil Imperial government. And it was only by turning to the Force that young Luke Skywalker accomplished his daring mission in the space battle over the Death Star.

Dr. Bill Bright, founder and president of Campus Crusade for Christ International, in his book, *A Movement of Miracles,* explained what it will take to save America:

"We, as individual Christians, are the ones who will determine whether or not we, as a nation, will fulfill our God-given role in history. We have the option of claiming the promise God gave to Solomon centuries ago: 'If my people, which are called by my name, shall humble themselves, and pray, and seek my face, and turn from their wicked ways; then will I hear from heaven, and will forgive their sin, and will heal their land' (2 Chronicles 7:14, *KJV*).

"We need to keep on believing, keep on humbling ourselves and keep on turning from all those sinful ways that hinder the working of the Holy Spirit. We need to keep on praying."

STAR WARS

Released by 20th Century-Fox

An Imperial stormtrooper, one of the fearsome soldiers of the Galactic Empire, fires at the fleeing Princess Leia.

Chapter 3

The Force of Star Wars

Young Luke Skywalker had never heard "the Force" mentioned by his Uncle Owen or Aunt Beru. Perhaps it was because the Force was the issue at the center of the galactic war that had spanned the better part of a decade. It had resulted in the death of Luke's father and thousands more Jedi Knights of the Old Republic. Now that Owen and Beru had the responsibility of raising Luke, they were not about to fill his head with thoughts about the Force—which could only lead to his answering the call of the rebellion that was already a small, distant voice in the recesses of his consciousness.

So when Obi-wan Kenobi, the last of the Jedi Knights, fondly mentioned the Force, Luke was immediately smitten with an obsession to learn and to join the rebellion against the evil Imperial government.

For Good or Evil

Kenobi brought up the subject of the Force quite by coincidence. Following their encounter with the mummy-clothed Tusken Raiders, better known as the Sandpeople, he explained how Luke's father had met his death at the hands of Darth Vader, a former student of Kenobi's who mastered the ways of the "dark side" of the Force, only to use its power for evil purposes. The Force, according to the theory of scientists, was an energy field generated by living things. Since uneducated early man was unable to deal with the Force on scientific terms, he sought supernatural explanations for it. The force was clearly a diety—a god— to these early people, and some of them even thought the Force controlled man's actions and not the other way around. Kenobi held this ancient view. When speaking of the Force, old Kenobi's eyes sparkled as if he were talking about a very dear old friend rather than an impersonal Force.

The Jedi Knights possessed the secret for tapping the limitless power of the Force, which gave them their special prowess as space warriors.

And if Luke Skywalker was to join Kenobi and the Alliance in their mission for the cause of the Republic, then he too would have to learn the ways of the Force.

The Search for the True Force

The search for the source of life and the explanation for the creation of the universe has gone on down through the ages. Anthropologists tell us that even the most primitive peoples, in their attempt to explain the mysteries of the universe, see the answers in supernatural forces. Generally, explanations for the existence of all things are found to fit in three basic categories of religious belief: the atheistic view, the pantheistic view and the theistic view. Now don't let these technical terms confuse you, because they are simple to understand.

The atheist (sometimes called materialist) believes in the existence of material things only—that which can be detected with the five senses of sight, hearing, feeling, tasting and smelling. In the mind of the atheist, there is no supernatural force in existence beyond the material universe. In other words, there is nothing spiritual, there are only things like rocks, trees and animals.

Similar to the atheistic view is that of

pantheism, which is the basis of most Eastern religions. The pantheist, like the atheist, believes in only material things. But, he sees a force in the material world—a divine force in the rocks and trees and animals.

Finally, the theistic view recognizes the material world but also finds a very real spiritual world. Polytheists believe in many gods, while monotheists believe in only one God. The Bible describes God as a single being—a divine force, if you will, with personality, infinite power and knowledge, and character. He alone is the creator of all things, the cause behind the existence of the creation. Because He is personal He has the ability to relate on a personal level with His creation, namely with human beings.

The Many Names of the True Force

We in America, because of our Judeo-Christian heritage, usually refer to this True Force as Jehovah or God, the one true God of the Bible. In the Old Testament we read of some of the many names of God. Let's become acquainted with these names, because they have much to say about the nature of God.

Elohim is a Hebrew word which is usually used in its plural form in reference to Almighty God. This plural form for the one God reminds us that He is three persons in one: God the Father, the Son and the Holy Spirit. The plural form enlarges upon the idea of God expressed in the singular, emphasizing the greatness of God.

Yahweh is usually translated as "Lord" (Master), although sometimes it is transliterated "Jehovah." It is the personal name of the living God of Israel.

Adonai is also a plural form, like *Elohim,* which shows God as a being full of life and power. It is translated "Lord," "Lord of lords," and "Lord of all the earth," indicating that God is the highest ruler of all. Everything is therefore subject to God, and man is His servant.

Jehovah-jireh, mentioned in the first book of the Bible, means "the Lord provides."[1] Here we see God as the great provider—One who meets the needs of His People.

Jehovah-nissi was the name Moses gave to a victory altar after defeating the Amalekites.[2] It means "the Lord is my banner." It is a small flag that an army rallies around and follows into combat. So if the Lord is a banner, troops rally around Him as He leads them into conflict. Can you think of anyone else you would rather follow into battle?

Jehovah-shalom is the name given by Gideon to the altar he built in honor to God.[3] It means "the Lord is peace." There are many references in the Bible where God promises to give His people peace. But the kind of peace the Lord gives is different from the peace found in worldly things; it is a peace within the soul.[4]

Jehovah-tsidkenu is the name by which the Son of God—the Messiah—is to be known.[5] It means "the Lord is our righteousness." The Bible tells us that God demands right actions and right thoughts from all men. But because of the imperfect nature of man, he is not always able to do what is right in God's sight. The result, because God is righteous, He will punish men for their wrongdoings. But, as we shall see in a later chapter, God, out of His love and mercy, provided His Son to be punished as a substitute for all who believe in Him. In this sense, the Lord has the ability to make all men righteous by forgiving them their wrongdoings and taking their punishment upon Himself.

Jehovah-shammah is the name given to the city of Ezekiels's vision, and means "the Lord is there."[6] This was a promise by

God that He would be with His people in the city. Indeed, the Lord is with His people wherever they might be, and will remain with them forever.[7] Long before people said, "The Force be with you," believers bid farewell with the phrase, "God be with you."

The Lord of hosts is different from the above names of God, in that this is a divine title. It is used in the Bible to show God as always being the Savior and Protector of His people.[8] The "hosts" are all the heavenly powers who stand ready to do as the Lord commands.

Lord God of Israel is another title and is used many times by the prophets of the Old Testament.[9] It always refers to the one true God who is worshiped by the people of Israel.

The Holy One of Israel was a favorite title for God with the prophet Isaiah (he used it twenty-nine times in his prophetic writings in the Bible). Similar to this are the titles, "the Mighty One of Israel"[10] and "the Strength (victory) of Israel."[11]

Ancient of days is the description by the prophet Daniel, who pictures God on His throne of judgment, judging the great world empires at the end of the age.[12]

A Living Being

The Bible always discusses the being of God in relation to His attributes, or character qualities. He is described as spirit, pure, moral, personal and having no beginning and no ending. He is the supreme mind and the source of all knowledge and wisdom for His creatures.

God is infinite in the sense that there is no limit to His knowledge or any other quality. Though a personal being, God is present throughout all His creation and is the ultimate and supreme Force.

What God Is Made Of

God's very being and His divine qualities are the same. This means that the substance of God *is* love, that He *is* all power, that He *is* all knowledge, that He *is* righteousness, that He *is* mercy, and so on.

To help us better understand the attributes of God, they can be classified in two groups—communicable and incommunicable, that is, attributes which can and cannot be transferred from God to man.

The communicable attributes include wisdom, goodness, righteousness, justice and love. We can actually have these qualities in our own lives; but, of course, in much lesser degree than God, because we are imperfect and He alone is perfect.

The incommunicable attributes of God are those which we cannot obtain in our lives because we are mortal. God possesses them because He is eternal and perfect.

These unique qualities of God include the following:

Self-existence. God is the sole cause for His own existence. He does not depend upon any force outside Himself.

Unchanging. His being, perfections, purposes and promises are all unchanging. He is the same yesterday, today and forever.[13]

All-knowing and all-presence. God's knowledge is part of His divine nature. He doesn't have to learn things as we do. He already knows all things! His knowledge is perfect as well as complete, and extends into the past as well as into the future. Because God is all-knowing, He must be in all places at all times—nothing is or takes place outside of His presence or knowledge.

All-powerful. God is the True Force. Within Him is concentrated the complete, supreme power that can create something out of nothing. God's power is totally creative. He is the Creator of the universe and all that is within it.

Eternal. God is not limited by time. He

has no beginning and no end. "I am," He said, showing that His all-presence is eternal.[14]

Holiness. The most distinctive attribute of God is His holiness. Only God is holy: nothing in His creation comes near holiness. What is the holiness of God? It is His intellectual and moral splendor; His ethical purity in delighting over good and hating all that is evil.

The Ways of the True Force

God is in control of all things—except the will of man. Since His knowledge is perfect in all things past and all things future, He does not have to wait for things to happen as we do. He planned them and they will happen just the way He planned.[15] Will His plans change? Hardly, because this would imply He lacked wisdom in planning in the first place, or lacked power in carrying out His plans. God's plans for all creation are explained in the Bible.

While God desires certain things from man, His desires are often disobeyed. He gave man a free will in order that man might worship Him out of his own desire and not because he is some kind of robot which is programmed. But, man, because he is not perfect like God, often wills to do those things which fall short of God's perfect standards. Such disobedience is called sin in the Bible, and the Ten Commandments clearly show how far short of perfection we all fall.[16] Because God is just, He punishes all sin.

Here is a real dilemma. Since "doing our own thing" results in sin, and since we are not capable of living up to God's perfect standards even when we try, is there no escape from God's judgment? I've got good news for you! Jesus Christ is God's "way out." The Bible explains it so well:

"For God so loved the world that He gave His only begotten Son, that whoever believes in Him should not perish, but have eternal life" (John 3:16, *NASB*).

True freedom, then, does not come in doing our own thing, but through faith in Jesus Christ.

More than undefinable energy, the True Force whom we know as the God of the Bible is a perfect being who created all things, who controls the destiny of the universe, and who desires that all men find freedom in His perfect will through belief in His Son, Jesus Christ.

STAR WARS
Released by 20th Century-Fox

Princess Leia (**Carrie Fisher**) defends herself against the Imperial attack aboard her Rebel Blockade Runner.

Chapter 4

The Fallen Star

The Republic, once like a mighty tree, able to withstand any kind of external attack, was beginning to rot, unnoticed, from the inside. No one questioned when the ambitious Senator Palpatine began his ascent to the Presidency. There were many restless, power-hungry individuals within the government and the commercial sector who quickly grasped the opportunity to support him in what some might call a conspiracy to take over the government. They knew their rewards would be great *if they succeeded.*

It was tragic that the once-respected Senator Palpatine began compromising values in small things, only to end up jeopardizing the future of the Republic because of his own ambition and greed.

The Quiet Takeover

With the help of his cronies in government and the world of commerce, Senator Palpatine succeeded in getting himself elected President of the Republic. Most people were so preoccupied with enjoying the good life that what happened in politics mattered little to them. Oh, there were no doubt some who saw and questioned what was happening. But their fears were quickly relieved when Palpatine promised to reunite the disaffected among the people and to restore the remembered glory of the Republic. So the *coup* of Senator Palpatine was quick and quiet.

Palpatine relished everything about being President—the power, the recognition, the wealth. Surrounded by yes-men, he began to fantasize himself as being a rather superhuman kind of person, able to always make right decisions and command the respect and admiration of his loyal subjects. As the fantasy grew and grew in his mind, he finally came upon the idea that would give him the ultimate satisfaction: to be Emperor.

What is an emperor? Historically, an emperor is a tyrant, a dictator, one who not only headed the government, but *was* the government. His word was law. Many of the Roman emperors, like Palpatine, had visualized themselves as something greater than human. Some of them went so far as to proclaim themselves gods and demanded that their subjects bow down in homage before them.

There is no proof that Palpatine instituted emperor worship, but that certainly must have crossed his mind for the future.

The Defeat of the Jedi Knights

The only thing which could have held the Emperor back from having his subjects worship him as god is the fact that the Jedi Knights, in addition to being the powerful warriors they were, were also the foundation of the Old Republic's body of religious devotees who were strongly committed to following the ways of the Force. Could it have been that the Emperor wanted them out of the way so that the citizens of the Republic would soon forget about the Force? This would make it much simpler to introduce emperor-worship again, at some future time.

Well, all that is, of course, speculation. But legend makes it quite clear that the Jedi Knights were exterminated through the treachery and deception of Palpatine and, especially, his henchman, Darth Vader. The guardians of justice in the galaxy were no more. And gone with them was the strong religious leadership which had been the foundation of the Republic for generations.

There were many citizens who refused to go along with the New Order. And many, no doubt, continued to follow the ways of the Force. To combat any open hostility to the new regime, the Imperial governors and bureaucrats prepared to institute a reign of terror among the disheartened worlds of the galaxy.

The Roots of Evil

The Emperor Palpatine and his betrayal of the public trust has an uncanny counterpart in reality. But, ironically, the time and place where all this really happened was, to paraphrase a popular line, in a world long ago, and far, far away. This we know: It all happened long before the earth was created.

The book of Job in the Old Testament gives us a glimpse of what things were like in those pre-earth days. Job, by the way, was a man who had many problems. Naturally, like many men when their troubles seemed overwhelming, Job began to question God's judgment. But God *quickly* began asking Job a series of questions that showed him he *obviously* didn't have *nearly* the wisdom it would take to judge God! It is from this line of questioning, though, that we learn some of the fascinating truths about the creation of the world and its surrounding universe:

"Then the Lord answered Job out of the whirlwind and said, 'Who is this that darkens counsel by words without knowledge? Now gird up your loins like a man, and I will ask you, and you instruct Me! Where were you when I laid the foundation of the earth! Tell Me, if you have understanding, who set its measurements since you know? Or who stretched the line on it? On what were its bases sunk? Or who laid its cornerstone, when the morning stars sang together, and all the sons of God shouted for joy?' " (Job 38:1-7, *NASB*).

The terms, "morning stars" and "sons of God," are often used in the Old Testament to identify heavenly beings. This passage shows us that angels were in God's presence when He created the earth. These spirit beings sang together and shouted with joy when God created the earth. There was total harmony in heaven and on the new earth. Here is pictured every being in heaven, happy in his role in God's kingdom.

Lucifer: Leader of Angels

One of these happy angels was Lucifer. The Bible describes him as having the highest position among the angels. We are introduced to him in the book of Ezekiel, where God addresses him as the "king of Tyre."

" 'Son of man, take up a lamentation over the king of Tyre, and say to him, "Thus says the Lord God, 'You had the seal of perfection, full of wisdom and perfect in beauty. You were in Eden, the garden of God; every precious stone was your covering; the ruby, the topaz, and the diamond; the beryl, the onyx, and the jasper; the lapis lazuli, the turquoise, and the emerald; and the gold, the workmanship of your settings and sockets, was in you. On the day that you were created they were prepared. You were the anointed cherub who covers; and I placed you there. You were on the holy mountain of God; you walked in the midst of the stones of fire. You were blameless in your ways from the day you created, until unrighteousness was found in you' " ' " (Ezekiel 28:12-15, *NASB*).

God loved Lucifer—His perfect creation, "full of wisdom and perfect in beauty." Lucifer was the wisest and most beautiful being in Eden, the perfect garden of God. He had been "on the holy mountain of God" and "walked in the midst of the stones of fire," two poetic descriptions of being in the holy presence of God.

Lucifer was the "anointed cherub who covers," which means he was the angel appointed by God to rank above and lead all the other angelic beings in heaven in praising and worshiping God. Every precious stone was used in his garments, as an indication of his high position.

Lucifer then was the greatest angel ever created by God. He had been a perfect creation, with unequaled beauty, wisdom, strength, authority and privilege.

The Father of Evil

Lucifer was "blameless" in his ways from the day he was created . . . but then he chose to do his own will rather than God's. The one who once was in charge of all the angels in heaven became the one who introduced evil into the universe. In a song of sorrow, recorded in the book of Isaiah, God mourns over this creature whom He had created and loved:

" 'How you have fallen from heaven, O star of the morning, son of the dawn! You have been cut down to the earth, you who have weakened the nations! But you said in your heart, "I will ascend to heaven; I will raise my throne above the stars of God, and I will sit on the mount of assembly in the recesses of the north. I will ascend above the heights of the clouds; and I will make myself like the Most High" ' " (Isaiah 14:12-14, *NASB*).

From the description in this passage, "O star of the morning, son of the dawn!" we see why God chose to call His greatest of all creations "Lucifer": The name means "the shining one." Quite possibly, his brilliance was patterned after God's own shining glory.

The Will to Worship the True Force

Why would God create a being who would turn against Him? Was this a mistake on God's part? Not at all.

In the previous chapter, we learned the ways of God's will. In some matters, the creation of the universe, for example, He determined that it would be done and it was done. Yet, we learned too that when it comes to man, God *desires* man to act and think in certain ways. But because man has a will of his own, he can choose to do what God desires of him, or he can do his own thing (which is sin).

Well, long before God created the first man, He created Lucifer and all the angels in heaven. And, He created them with the ability to choose to worship Him and follow His perfect ways, or go their own way. God created them with their own wills. Ironically, Lucifer wasn't satisfied with just being the highest ranking angel in heaven, the most beautiful and most wise of all created beings! "I will make myself like the Most High (God)," he said. "I will ... I will ... I will." Lucifer chose not to follow God, but to go his own way.

Lucifer said these things in his heart. *In his heart!* That was where sin originated—in the heart of Lucifer. And in his heart there were what have become known as the five "I wills." They show a definite departure from Lucifer's early determination to follow God's will to his later decision to follow his own will. Lucifer wasn't happy with his position in the realm of God. He wanted to take over God's position and be worshiped and praised by all the creation. He wanted to be God!

The Deception of Sin

Lucifer became so blinded by the sin in his heart that he couldn't realize the simplest of all truths: There is but one God and He and only He is worthy of praise and worship.

No, Lucifer could never rise above God. In fact, he no longer was permitted by God to lead the angels, as he used to do, in worship and praise. No, it was just the opposite now. The Bible says Lucifer became a blasphemer, which means he verbally attacked God's holy character. But he went beyond that. He led a great rebellion in the universe against God.

In a vision from God, the apostle John was shown what happened when Lucifer rebelled:

"And there was war in heaven. Michael and his angels fought against the dragon (Lucifer), and the dragon and his angels fought back. But he was not strong enough, and they lost their place in heaven. The great dragon was hurled down—that ancient serpent called the devil or Satan, who leads the whole world astray. He was hurled to the earth, and his angels with him" (Revelation 12:7-9).

Remember that Lucifer, who later was called Satan, had been the leader of all the angels, so when he rebelled against God, he still held a great deal of influence over the angelic realm. As a result, one-third of the countless multitudes of angels in heaven followed him in this revolt against God.[1] Now, these angels had free wills, too. They could choose whether to worship God or follow Lucifer into sin. And, of course, they made the wrong decision.

Though Lucifer became the first sinful creature, he still possessed his beauty, wisdom and strength. Of course, he lost his position of authority. But worse, he had broken off his relationship with God forever.

Lucifer and his fallen angels were now in sinful rebellion against God. The once pure universe was now seriously contaminated with evil.

Lucifer's Judgment

Because God is perfectly just, the crimes committed by Lucifer and his fallen angels had to be judged and punished. Now God has a very simple code of criminal law: Any sin, no matter how small, is punishable by eternal death—everlasting separation from God!—and this applies to men as well as to angels.

In order to separate Lucifer and the

fallen angels from Himself, God created a place for them which the Bible calls hell.[2]

Following the outbreak of the rebellion in heaven, God changed the name of Lucifer to Satan, the devil, the evil one. "Satan" means "the resister or adversary," and "devil" means "the accuser and slanderer."

Though judgment has been passed by God on Satan and the fallen angels, the sentence has not yet been served. Meanwhile, Satan has one tireless ambition, to defeat the plans and purposes of God. He began this evil campaign shortly after the creation of man in the garden of Eden. He deceived Eve into sinning and she then persuaded Adam to deliberately sin.[3]

The Ruler of This World

The sin committed by Adam and Eve was an act of direct disobedience—open rebellion—toward God. It broke their perfect fellowship with God and placed them under the control of Satan, who is the father of sin.[4]

Adam and Eve had been given authority over the world and everything in it by God.[5] But now, because of sin, they brought that authority to rule over the earth with them as they came under Satan's control. This way, Satan usurped the rule over the world, and the whole earth now lies under the domination of Satan.[6] In fact, the Bible calls him, among other things, the "prince of this world."[7]

Satan goes by many other titles, as well: Abaddon, Accuser, Adversary, Dragon or the Serpent of the bottomless pit, Apollyon, Belial, Beelzebub, Murderer, Prince of the Devils, Prince of the power of the air, and the god of this age.[8]

As the god of this age, Satan holds men in an iron grip of sin. It is a grip that only can be broken when a person places his faith and life in the hands of Jesus Christ. But a new age is coming, a time of wonderful, perfect bliss for Christ's believers. It will also be a time of unimaginable horror for Satan and his followers.

The result of sin by the first humans—Adam and Eve—is seen in the sin nature which is found in every person who ever lived or ever will live. While angels were created with perfect natures, man is born with a sin nature. An angel has the self-determination to sin, but men and women are born sinners and therefore condemned from birth. And, as we have already discussed, man can choose to sin, as well.

"That's not fair," you say. "Man doesn't have a chance against sin." But, you must remember that God is perfect. Out of His perfect love for man He has provided a way for man to defeat his three enemies, Satan, sin and death. That plan for victory is being worked out right now on planet earth, and mankind finds itself right in the middle of the most colossal battle the universe has ever seen: the battle for men's souls between Satan and his evil spirits and God and his angelic hosts.

This battle has been fought in every generation since the first generation of man. Countless illustrations have been drawn to depict this classic battle, and *Star Wars* is but the latest entry.

The galactic wars in the movie are really religious wars: The people of the Alliance, who believe in and follow the ways of the Force, are pitted against the satanic emperor Palpatine, Grand Moff Tarkin, Darth Vader, and all the other "fallen stars" of the Old Republic.

The Bible tells us there is a bitter conflict raging throughout the spiritual universe, and it's no secret to anyone that a fierce battle between the forces of good and the forces of evil is being fought on planet earth today. This is a very real and a very personal battle, and it doesn't take much honest introspection within the recesses of our own minds and hearts to find evil thoughts lurking there, or to observe our own behavior and see sinful acts being committed.

The only way for us to overcome the evil power of Satan and his fallen angels is to become children of the True Force and learn to follow His ways.

STAR WARS
Released by 20th Century-Fox

Artoo-Detoo and See-Threepio are on Owen Lars' homestead on Tatooine.

Chapter 5

The Creatures from Other Worlds

Mos Eisley was the most wretched settlement in the universe, where only the extreme, disreputable types of creatures hung out. It was where Luke and Kenobi visited in search of a starship pilot who would ferry them to Alderaan, with no questions asked!

The town's strange assortment of beings strolled the streets, hawking what was mostly contraband wares, or looking for good deals. Others gathered in the shadows to plot smuggling runs, and other such business, behind the backs of Imperial stormtroopers.

Nowhere in town was there a greater concentration of weird specimens from throughout the galaxies than at the sleazy cantina. The humans who hung out there were motley enough, but they were the minority, being surrounded by a nightmare of creatures—some with only one eye and others with thousands, some with scales and others with fur, and others with ripply skin that changed consistency as their feelings changed. Tentacles and claws and paws clutched a variety of drinking utensils. These oversized bugs and incredible reptile-like beings drank, ate and smoked from strange instruments, and "talked" in every conceivable kind of space gibberish. Off in a corner some giant outer space jitterbugs constituted a jazz band providing music by which to do whatever space creatures do in such places!

Judging from the looks and actions of this space menagerie, Luke, Kenobi, Han Solo (the pilot of the *Millennium Falcon*), and Chewbacca were the only good guys in the place.

Stranger Than Make-Believe

Strange as these *Star Wars* creatures were, in the real world there are stranger ones still. The world might not have insectoids and reptilians and the nightmare versions of Sesame Street monsters, but a quick scan through an illustrated encyclopedia will reveal all sorts of odd animals, insects and plants. Then consider the kinds of beasts that used to roam the planet earth—the dinosaurs and the giant insects!

But there is yet another, even stranger dimension of beings in the real world: one, interestingly, alluded to in *Star Wars*—the spirit world.

In an earlier chapter, we discussed the person of God, and in another, Satan. We know from the Bible that both are surrounded by spirit beings. Angels are of God's realm and demons are the evil spirits that follow Satan.

Satan continues to lead the great rebellion that is shaking the universe, involving both the world we live in and the spirit world around us. All creation—God's angelic realm, Satan and his demons, and, yes, even we humans are the combatants in this eerie but real battle for men's souls.

The Unseen Dimension

Are angels and demons real? Do they have any influence on our everyday lives? You had better believe they do! If we had the ability to see into this other dimension of the spirit world we would be astounded at the overwhelming number of spirit beings surrounding us! They can see us, but we, of course, can't see them.

The word "angel" comes from the

Greek word *angelos,* and means "a messenger of God." The word can mean both a spiritual messenger or a mortal one, depending on the context.

Sometimes angels are called "sons of God"[1] and "holy ones."[2] Angels were created as perfect beings. However, as we noted earlier, they have free wills, which means they can be tempted into sin. Consequently, angels can be good angels, possibly good, or fallen; the name itself doesn't necessarily mean good.[3]

You have probably heard about "guardian angels." Well, God does use angels to relate to mortals. He sends them to us with specific commands and greetings and help in time of need.[4] He sends them on missions to provide military assistance,[5] and in some cases to engage in active combat.[6] Angels, then, can be very warlike,[7] and have been known to smite and kill evildoers at God's command.[8]

Gabriel and Michael

While angels have personalities only two of them are mentioned by proper names in the Bible: Gabriel and Michael. Gabriel is the spokesman of God who explained the meaning of prophetic visions to the prophet Daniel.[9] Michael is the guardian angel of the nation of Israel, and is called the "archangel," which means "chief angel."[10]

Scripture suggests that there are various orders of spirit beings in God's presence. The prophet Isaiah mentions celestial creatures called seraphim and cherubim. These are multi-winged spirit beings whose responsibility it is to lead the angelic hosts in worship and praise of God.[11]

The cherubim each have four faces—those of a man, a lion, an ox, and an eagle—and four wings. Seraphim have six wings each. In the book of Revelation, we are told about four living creatures who surround the throne of God. They closely resemble the cherubim of Isaiah, yet have an additional characteristic mentioned: they are full of eyes in front and behind. Judging from the appearance of these beings, they would fit in very comfortably with the crowd at the cantina in *Star Wars!*

These strange-looking beings suggest the praise and adoration given to God by His entire creation, and they represent angelic beings who are used by God in executing His rule and divine will throughout the universe. Twenty-four elders, another order of angelic being, share in this responsibility.

Devils, Demons and Evil Spirits

The multitude of angels that were persuaded to follow Lucifer in his rebellion against God are found with new names throughout Scripture: demons, devils and evil spirits.

These evil spirit beings, which are hostile to God and men, are mentioned throughout the Bible, especially in the New Testament. Beelzebub, another name for Satan, is their "prince."[12]

Demon possession is not mentioned in the Old Testament. It is cited only once in the book of Acts and not referred to at all in any of the epistles of the New Testament.[13] This seems to indicate that demon possession was present predominantly during the early ministry of Jesus Christ. But, at the end of the age, according to Scripture, demons will be very active, carrying out the evil plot of Satan against Christ and men.[14]

People have become so fascinated with demons that Hollywood has had windfall profits from such demon-oriented motion pictures as *Rosemary's Baby*, *The Exorcist* and *The Omen*.

These demons possess strong evil powers that can be overcome only by forces mightier than human. Jesus Christ, exercising the power of God, was able to cast out demons when they possessed individuals.[15] He gave His disciples the same power and authority over all demons and to cure diseases.[16] Others received this same power and authority, and today many people claim to be able to cast out demons through the power of the Spirit of God.[17]

Battle Lines are Drawn

So there is the roster of combatants in this religious war to end all religious wars. And it is accelerating swiftly toward its certain climax at the end of the age. It's Satan and his evil spirits against God and His heavenly host *and* man. Satan has already embarked upon an all-out battle to disrupt God's plans for the future. While Satan certainly knows he has lost the war, he realizes that he and his demons can continue to work out their contempt for God by leading men away from Jesus Christ and into eternal hopelessness.

STAR WARS
Released by 20th Century-Fox

Jawas, the rodent-like scrap collectors of Tatooine, weld a small control disk onto the side of Artoo-Detoo.

Chapter 6

The Morning Star

Obi-wan Kenobi is a classic hero in every sense of the word. Once a great general of the Jedi Knights, but cast into obscurity as a result of the galactic wars, he lived out the later years of his life as an ordinary person in the desert regions of Tatooine. But he had an appointment with destiny. It was triggered when he came to the rescue of Luke Skywalker. Luke had been looking for his new and wayward mechanical Artoo-Detoo, when he encountered the Tusken Raiders. He would have been killed by these desert bandits had Kenobi not come to drive them away.

Out of that encounter, a relationship developed between Kenobi and Luke which set the stage for a daring mission that would change the course of life for everyone in the galactic system.

The Power of the Force

Ben Kenobi had had a distinguished career in the Jedi Knights, one characterized by his amazing use of the power of the Force for the good of others. This won for him deep reverence on the part of his fellow Jedi Knights, as well as respect from his foes. His mere presence sent terror racing through the hearts of the Tusken Raiders (Do Tusken Raiders have hearts?), and Darth Vader cautioned Governor Tarkin not to underestimate Kenobi's skill in utilizing the awesome power of the Force.

But now Kenobi was literally passing on the sword to the next generation, along with all his knowledge about the Force. Young Luke Skywalker became Kenobi's single disciple for learning how to appropriate the power of the Force. Luke's adventuresome spirit and ability to grasp the ways of the Force quickly led Kenobi to compare him favorably with his late father, also once a Jedi Knight, whom Darth Vader had caused to be killed through his treachery and betrayal.

Sometimes, it almost seemed as though Kenobi himself were the Force. This was especially so when he manipulated the thoughts of his foes or faced them with light saber in hand. He wielded the slender shaft of pure energy in such a way as to suggest that he and this incomparable weapon of the Jedi Knights were one.

The Morning Star

The relationship of Kenobi to the Force has an important parallel in the real world. It centers in the person of Jesus Christ, poetically called "the bright morning star" in the Bible.[1] Just as the make-believe Kenobi of *Star Wars* had the power of the Force within him, the real person of Jesus Christ has the power of the True Force within Him—God! Only more: Jesus Christ *is* God. He once walked the earth as the God-man, and now reigns at the right hand of God the Father in heaven.

While Kenobi was wise in the ways of the Force, Jesus Christ, even as a youth, astounded the rabbis with His wisdom and knowledge of God. Not to mention the numerous miracles He performed! Just as Kenobi taught his former disciple, Darth Vader, and his new one, Luke Skywalker, in the ways of the Force, Jesus Christ taught His disciples (and multitudes more) the ways of the True Force, Almighty God.

The Tusken Raiders fled in terror at the sight of Kenobi, and so did Satan's demons flee from Jesus, the Son of God, so great was His power and authority over them.

The Name Above All Names

The name of Jesus Christ is known to practically everyone, yet only in the last few years has His name become widely associated with personalities in government, business, entertainment, and even with former criminals.

Washington, D.C. and much of the skeptical press wouldn't believe it when former Watergate figure Chuck Colson announced he had become spiritually "born again" through receiving Jesus Christ as his personal Savior and Lord.

President Jimmy Carter has said the most important person in his life is Jesus Christ.

Walt Disney star Dean Jones turned his life over to Jesus Christ in a lonely motel room after finding nothing but frustration and emptiness in his desperate search for happiness and purpose in career, money and alcohol.

And former Black Panther leader Eldridge Cleaver returned from self-exile to shock the world that he, too, had become a Christian!

No other person in history has had so

great an impact upon mankind, so that history itself is divided around the date of His birth: B.C. (Before Christ) and A.D. (*anno domini*—"in the year of our Lord").

The Life That Changed the World

Jesus Christ was born in the obscure village of Bethlehem in Judea (Northern Judea). He worked in His earthly father's carpenter shop until, at age thirty, He began preaching to Jews and Gentiles alike throughout Palestine. More than nineteen centuries have passed since His birth, and religions and religious cults have come and gone, but Jesus Christ remains the central figure in history. There has never been a government or any leader who has come close to having the impact on the world as that of Jesus Christ.

He Existed Before Time

Though Jesus Christ was born of the virgin Mary nearly 2,000 years ago, He is much older than that. The Bible explains to us that He lived *before* He appeared on earth as a baby!

Jesus Himself tells us that He is the Eternal One from heaven, that He has always existed and always will exist: "For I have come down from heaven not to do my will but to do the will of him who sent me . . . before Abraham was born, I am! . . . And now, Father, glorify me in your presence with the glory I had with you before the world began" (John 6:38; 8:58; 17:5).[2]

The disciples of Jesus Christ also claimed He was the Eternal One from heaven. In the beginning of the Gospel according to John, we read about the "Word," which in the original Greek is *logos.*[3] This word means thought, concept, and the expression or utterance of that thought. Jesus is the expression of the mind of God. "The Word became flesh," explains John in his narrative, "and lived for a while among us. We have seen his glory, the glory of the one and only Son, who came from the Father, full of grace and truth" (John 1:14).

In verse 1, "In the beginning," indicates that Jesus existed before anything else! "He was with God" shows that He is a distinct person and that He enjoys eternal fellowship with God. "And the Word was God" clearly explains that Jesus Christ is God. All that God is, the Word is too! Jesus made the point plain to His disciple, Philip: "I am in the Father and the Father is in me" (John 14:11).

The universe and everything in it point to the preexistence of Jesus Christ. "Through him all things were made," wrote the apostle John. "Without him nothing was made that has been made. . . . He was in the world, and though the world was made through him, the world did not recognize him" (John 1:3,10).

Predictions of His Coming

Bible scholars have counted more than 300 prophecies of Christ's coming in the Old Testament. Because of our limited space in this book, we can look at only a few of them, as follows:

The first book of the Bible (Genesis) carries the first prophecy about the coming Messiah, His being born of a woman and His triumph over Satan.[4]

Don't let the word "Messiah" confuse you. It's the Hebrew word for "anointed one," just as "Christ" is the Greek word with the same meaning. The Old Testament was written in Hebrew and the New Testament in Greek, thus "Messiah" and "Christ," both of which refer to Jesus of Nazareth.

The coming Messiah is seen as a great prophet.[5] Moreover, He was seen in the Psalms as the coming Messiah-King, who would rule in Zion and be God's Son.[6] The prophet Isaiah pictured Him as a man, as God, as the King of Israel, and as the Savior who would die for the sins of the world.[7] Though He is eternal God, He was to be born in the little town of Bethlehem, of a virgin, according to prophecy.[8]

When taken in its whole, the Old Testament prophecies of the coming Messiah pointed to Him as being far more than a man. He was to be the God-man.

Just as Obi-wan Kenobi's life and death changed the course of history in that make-believe galactic struggle of the distant past, so too has the life and death and resurrection of the living Christ changed the course of history for the better.

STAR WARS
Released by 20th Century-Fox

Chewbacca, the hundred year old Wookie, co-pilots the Millennium Falcon, a Corellian pirate starship.

Chapter 7

The Treacherous Betrayal

Darth Vader had been a close friend of Obi-wan Kenobi, his former mentor in the Jedi Knights. Those were the days when the Republic was at the height of its glory and the Jedis protected the rights of all beings in the Galactic Empire in the name of the Force. More than any other disciple of Kenobi's, Darth had a penchant for quickly grasping difficult galactic war strategy and intergalactic political concepts. Above all, Darth developed a deep respect for the power of the Force and all who knew its ways.

In time, Darth himself became extremely knowledgeable in the ways of the Force and adroit in ways of appropriating its power. Judging from Kenobi's sincere interest in teaching Luke Skywalker the ways of the Force, it isn't difficult to imagine how fond he must have been of Darth Vader in those early days before the Dark Lord turned to evil. Sadly, Darth turned out to be Kenobi's worst failure.

Obsession for Power

Despite Darth Vader's brilliance and talents and mastery over the ways of the Force, his character had one serious flaw: the lack of moral value.

When the New Order was in its early stages, it became apparent to Darth that the Jedi Knights would have to be eliminated and that their days were numbered. So he switched allegiance and began using the power of the Force within him for evil purposes, in a conspiracy to help the corrupt Palpatine to seize control of the government, and then the very universe itself. Apparently, Darth was so obsessed for more and more power that he was eager and willing to join evil forces to get what he wanted.

An Ominous Name

The name "Darth Vader" has an ominous, if not familiar evil ring to it. Perhaps it is because it so closely sounds like "dark invader." And a dark invader Darth is. Black as his protective armor and grotesque breath mask are, the darkness in his evil mind and heart is blacker still. Using his power of the Force for evil, he eventually led the black-armored Imperial guards and white-armored stormtroopers on many invasions into the domain of the Republic, murdering, plundering and destroying all that was once good.

The Betrayer

It was inevitable that in Darth's lust for power he would have to deal with the most powerful of the Jedi Knights, the one who was blocking his evil quest. That Jedi was the father of Luke Skywalker. While the story was never quite clear as to how Darth brought about his death, it was commonly agreed upon it was through betrayal and treachery, which was Darth's way. Even Kenobi wasn't quite sure about the details of his death, but told young Luke enough to instill in him a spirit of revenge that was adequate for Luke to decide to fight for the preservation of the Old Republic, following in his father's footsteps.

Darth Vader had betrayed his fellow citizens of the Republic and had broken his oath as a Jedi Knight to uphold what is morally good through the power of the Force.

As the *Star Wars* adventure raced on toward its tension-filled climax, we found Darth face-to-face with a powerful Jedi Knight once again. This one, however, was the last and most powerful one of them all, the one whom he had perhaps betrayed the most, Obi-wan Kenobi!

Darth Vader represented the dark power of evil and Obi-wan Kenobi represented the forces of good. The confrontation was high in symbolism and many observers saw it as the classic struggle between good and evil—the good guy against the bad guy. It is the predominant theme in the movies, where the bad guys always wear black and the good ones always wear white.

And now, here was the Dark Lord, towering high in his black semi-armor and hideous black breath mask, his black steel helmet bearing a striking resemblance to the familiar steel pots of Hitler's stormtroopers. Darth was totally evil, and everything about his presence left no question about it. Kenobi, on the other hand, possessed many good qualities because of his relationship with the Force—peace, submission, warmth and altruism. He even wore white robes, which gave him a saintly kind of appearance. Indeed, it was a confrontation between good and evil!

Another Disciple, Another Betrayer

Perhaps the greatest truth seen in this aspect of the parable of *Star Wars* is the betrayal of Jesus Christ by one of His trusted disciples, Judas Iscariot.

Jesus had been traveling the countryside with His disciples, performing miracles to testify to His claim that He was the Son of God. Many people were placing their faith in Him and this greatly disturbed the chief priests and the Pharisees. They called a meeting of the Sanhedrin to deal with the problem:

" 'What are we accomplishing?' they asked. 'Here is this man performing many miraculous signs. If we let him go on like this, everyone will put his trust in him, and then the Romans will come and take away both our place (or temple) and our nation.'

"Then one of them, named Caiaphas, who was high priest that year, spoke up, 'You know nothing at all! You do not realize that it is better for you that one man die for the people than that the whole nation perish.'

"He did not say this on his own, but as high priest that year he prophesied that Jesus would die for the Jewish nation, and not only for that nation but also for the scattered children of God, to bring them together and make them one. So from that day on they plotted to take his life. . . . The chief priests and Pharisees had given orders that if anyone found out where Jesus was, he should report it so that they might arrest him" (John 11:45-53,57).

Judas, who was manager of the meager finances of the band of disciples and their leader, was so tempted for wealth that he allowed Satan to possess his soul, and agreed to lead the chief priests and Pharisees to Jesus.[1]

" 'He who shares my bread has lifted up his heel against me,' " Jesus told His disciples, astounding them. " 'I am telling you now before it happens, so that when it does happen you will believe that I am he (God). . . . I tell you the truth, one of you is going to betray me.'

"His disciples stared at one another, at a loss to know which of them he meant. One of them, the disciple whom Jesus loved, was reclining next to him. Simon Peter motioned to this disciple and said, 'Ask him which one he means.' Leaning back against Jesus, he asked him, 'Lord, who is it?' Jesus answered, 'It is the one to whom I will give this piece of bread when I have dipped it in the dish.' Then, dipping the piece of bread, he gave it to Judas Iscariot, son of Simon. As soon as Judas took the bread, Satan entered into him. 'What you are about to do, do quickly,' Jesus told him, but no one at the meal understood why Jesus said this to him" (John 13:18-28).

The Garden of Betrayal

Jesus had just finished praying for a lengthy period. He left the place where He was and took His disciples with Him across the Kidron Valley. There was an olive grove on the other side, and Jesus and His disciples went into it. The Bible tells us how the betrayal of Jesus was carried out:

"Now Judas, who betrayed him, knew the place, because Jesus had often met there with his disciples. So Judas came to the grove, guiding a detachment of soldiers and some officials from the chief priests and Pharisees. They were carrying torches, lanterns and weapons.

"Jesus, knowing all that was going to happen to him, went out and asked them, 'Who is it you want?'

" 'Jesus of Nazareth,' they replied.

" 'I am he,' Jesus said. (And Judas the traitor was standing there with them.)

When Jesus said, 'I am he,' they drew back and fell to the ground.

"Again he asked them, 'Who is it you want?'

"And they said, 'Jesus of Nazareth.'

" 'I told you that I am he,' Jesus answered. 'If you are looking for me, then let these men go.' This happened so that the words he had spoken would be fulfilled: 'I have not lost one of those you gave me.'

"Then Simon Peter, who had a sword, drew it and struck the high priest's servant, cutting off his right ear. (The servant's name was Malchus.)

"Jesus commanded Peter, 'Put your sword away! Shall I not drink the cup the Father has given me?'

"Then the detachment of soldiers with its commander and the Jewish officials arrested Jesus" (John 18:2-12).

Satan's evil plot to destroy the Son of God was moving rapidly ahead. But would it work?

STAR WARS

Released by 20th Century-Fox

Ben Kenobi (Alec Guinness), once a great warrior in the Old Republic, is now an outlaw in the Tatooine mountains.

Chapter 8

The Supreme Sacrifice

Since Obi-wan Kenobi had the power of the Force within him, why didn't he just lob off the gargoyle-like head of Darth Vader? Why did he just smile that all-knowing smile and bring his light saber to the neutral, formal position of a salute? It was because he knew he had to die!

Kenobi's sacrificial death momentarily drew the attention of the Imperial troops and allowed Princess Leia and her rescuers to flee in the *Millennium Falcon*. Had it not been for this, the cause of the Alliance would have been lost forever. Men would have continued to live in fear and bondage under the evil Imperial government.

The Night of Trials
Jesus Christ knew He had to die, too. His appointment at Calvary was part of

God's divine plan to redeem men from the curse of sin, Satan and death.

Following His arrest, Jesus, His hands bound, was tried several times in an ordeal that lasted throughout the night. First, he was taken to the house of Annas, the father-in-law of Caiaphas, the high priest for that year. But Annas evidently felt the charges against Jesus were weak, and decided it was politically expedient to turn Jesus over to Caiaphas.

Caiaphas, in turn, had Jesus taken to the palace of the Roman governor, Pilate, for trial. But since the chief priests and Pharisees were vague about their charges against Jesus, Pilate told them, " 'Take him yourselves and judge him by your own law' " (John 18:31).

But the Jews objected, reminding Pilate they had no authority under Roman law to execute criminals. Then Pilate went back to where Jesus was and questioned Him:

" 'Are you the king of the Jews?'

" 'Is that your own idea,' Jesus asked, 'or did others talk to you about me?'

" 'Do you think I am a Jew?' Pilate replied. 'It was your people and your chief priests who handed you over to me. What is it you have done?'

"Jesus said, 'My kingdom is not of this

world. If it were, my servants would fight to prevent my arrest by the Jews. But now my kingdom is from another place.'

" 'You are a king, then!' said Pilate.

"Jesus answered, 'You are right in saying I am a king. In fact, for this reason I was born, and for this I came into the world, to testify to the truth. Everyone on the side of truth listens to me.'

" 'What is truth?' Pilate asked. With this he went out again to the Jews and said, 'I find no basis for a charge against him. But it is your custom for me to release to you one prisoner at the time of the Passover. Do you want me to release "the king of the Jews"?'

"They shouted back, 'No, not him! Give us Barabbas!' " (John 18:33-40).

Sentenced to Be Executed

Then Pilate ordered his soldiers to flog Jesus. This they did, and also twisted together a crown of thorns and placed it on His head. They wrapped a purple robe around Him and mocked Him, calling Him the "king of the Jews."

Morning came and Pilate took Jesus before the people and explained to them that he found no basis for a charge against Him. But as soon as the the chief priests and other Jewish officials saw Him, they began chanting, "Crucify! Crucify!"

Undeterred, Pilate insisted the Jews take Jesus and crucify Him, because he wanted nothing to do with the matter.

Then the Jews explained to Pilate that since Jesus said He was the Son of God, Jewish law dictated that He should be killed.

Pilate was on the spot—and afraid. So he took Jesus back into his quarters and questioned Him some more. But Jesus said nothing.

" 'Do you refuse to speak to me?' Pilate said. "Don't you realize I have power either to free you or to crucify you?'

"Jesus answered, 'You have no power over me that was not given to you from above. Therefore the one who handed me over to you is guilty of a greater sin.'

"From then on, Pilate tried to set Jesus free, but the Jews kept shouting, 'If you let this man go, you are no friend of Caesar. Anyone who claims to be a king opposes Caesar' " (John 19:10-12).

The Execution

At last, Pilate turned Jesus over to the Jews to be crucified. Carrying His own cross, Jesus was escorted by Roman soldiers to "The Place of the Skull," which was called *Golgotha* in Arabic. There, the soldiers nailed Jesus to a cross that was placed between two others who were being crucified.

Pilate had a notice prepared and attached to the cross, which read, "Jesus of Nazareth, the King of the Jews." The soldiers who crucified Jesus took His clothes, dividing them into four shares, one for each of them. Since His undergarment was seamless and they didn't want to tear it, they decided by lot who would get it.

This was all done in literal fulfillment of the ancient prophecies in Scripture which said, "They divide my garments among them, and for my clothing they cast lots" (Psalm 22:18, *NASB*).

A Cruel Death

Crucifixion is a slow, agonizing form of execution. For Jesus, it was no less agonizing than for anyone else, because He was a man, as well as God.

Several prophecies were literally fulfilled as Jesus hung, dying on that cross. He said He was thirsty, and was given vinegar. And since the next day was a special Sabbath, the Jews did not want the bodies of the three men left on the crosses. So they asked Pilate to have the legs of the men broken, the shock of which would bring about quick death, and the bodies taken down.

The legs of the two men crucified side-by-side with Jesus were broken by the soldiers. But when Pilate's men came to Jesus, they knew He was already dead, and so they did not break His legs. Instead, one of them pierced the side of Jesus with a spear, causing a sudden flow of blood and water.

These incredibly detailed events had been prophesied many years earlier and recorded in the Scriptures. "Not one of His bones will be broken" (Psalm 34:20, *NASB*), and "They will look on [the One] they have pierced" (Zechariah 12:10, *NASB*). But the most striking prophecy concerning the death of Christ was recorded by the prophet Isaiah some 700 years before the crucifixion:

He was despised and forsaken of men,
A man of sorrows, and acquainted with
    grief;
And like one from whom men hide
    their face,
He was despised, and we did not esteem
    Him.

Surely our griefs He Himself bore,
And our sorrows He carried;
Yet we ourselves esteemed Him stricken,
Smitten of God, and afflicted.
But He was pierced through for our
    transgressions,
He was crushed for our iniquities;
The chastening for our well-being fell
    upon Him,
And by His scourging we are healed.
All of us like sheep have gone astray,
Each of us has turned to his own way;
But the Lord has caused the iniquity of
    us all
To fall on Him.

He was oppressed and He was afflicted,
Yet He did not open His mouth;
Like a lamb that is led to slaughter,
And like a sheep that is silent before its
    shearers,
So He did not open His mouth.
By oppression and judgment He was
    taken away;
And as for His generation, who con-
    sidered
That He was cut off out of the land of
    the living,
For the transgression of my people to
    whom the stroke was due?

His grave was assigned to be with
    wicked men,
Yet with a rich man in His death;
Although He had done no violence,
Nor was there any deceit in His mouth.
    (Isaiah 53:3-10, *NASB*)

The Meaning of the Cross

The Bible tells us there are at least eleven reasons why Jesus Christ died: (1) to free men from the condemnation of the Law;[1] (2) to defeat Satan and his power of death;[2] (3) to begin the new agreement between God and men for their salvation;[3] (4) to pay the penalty for all sins committed by men in all times past;[4] (5) to pay the penalty for all the sins of mankind, past, present and future;[5] (6) to break Satan's power of sin over men;[6] (7) to demonstrate God's love for men;[7] (8) to fulfill God's will;[8] (9) to show that God is righteous;[9] (10) to purify the Church;[10] and (11) to bring those who believe back into fellowship with Himself.[11]

Those are a lot of reasons for dying! We can see that the death of Jesus Christ was not the result of some unfortunate string of circumstances. It was part of God's perfect, eternal plan. Jesus *had* to die!

Understanding Death

Death is part of God's punishment for man's sins. We are told in Genesis 2:17 that God's holiness demands that sin be punished. Death is more than just physical separation of life from the body, it is the spiritual separation of life from God! The apostle Paul wrote to the Christians in Rome:

"Sin entered the world through one man, and death through sin, and in this way death came to all men, because all sinned. . . . the wages of sin is death, but the gift of God is eternal life through Christ Jesus our Lord" (Romans 5:12; 6:23).

Because of sin, men are born spiritually dead, that is spiritually separated from God. So when a man who is not a Christian dies, life is separated from his body, but his spirit, since birth, has already been separated from God, and he dies spiritually dead. Such a person is already under the authority of Satan and will therefore spend eternity with him in hell.

But Christians, at the moment of belief in Christ, become spiritually alive. They are spiritually "born again," we read in John 3, through the indwelling of the Holy Spirit of God. Jesus said we must be "born again" in order to enter the kingdom of heaven.

So, when a Christian dies, life is separated from his body, but since he now has an everlasting spiritual life, there is no separation from God. At the moment of physical death, a Christian's soul is immediately in the presence of Jesus Christ.

This is the promise of Christ:

"For God so loved the world that he gave his one and only Son, that whoever believes in him shall not perish but have everlasting life. . . . Whoever believes in him is not condemned, but whoever does not believe stands condemned already because he has not believed in the name of God's one and only Son" (John 3:16,18).[12]

The apostle John explained that all who believe have eternal life even before they die: "God has given us eternal life, and this life is in his Son. He who has the Son has life; he who does not have the Son of God does not have life. I write these things to you who believe in the name of the Son of God so that you may know that you have eternal life" (1 John 5:11-13).

Now here is an interesting thing about physical death. The Bible tells us about a time which is coming when Jesus Christ will return and all His believers who had died—that is, life had separated from their physical bodies, but their souls are with Him—will receive new, supernatural or glorified bodies. The apostle Paul explained this in his first letter to the Christians at Corinth:

"We shall not all sleep [remain physically dead], but we shall all be changed—in a flash, in the twinkling of an eye, at the last trumpet. For the trumpet will sound, the dead will be raised imperishable, and we shall be changed. For the perishable must clothe itself with the imperishable, and the mortal with immortality. . . . Then the saying that is written will come true: 'Death has been swallowed up in victory' " (1 Corinthians 15:51-54). This subject is expanded upon by Paul in 1 Thessalonians 4. Nonbelievers will be resurrected from the dead, too, at the time of God's "great white throne" judgment at the end of Christ's thousand-year reign on earth. But because of their sin, they will be cast into an eternally burning lake of fire along with Satan. You can read about this in Revelation 20.

The Perfect Substitute

Since death is God's punishment for sin, and since Jesus had never committed a sin, He should not have had to die.[13] He did it only because of His perfect love for man.

Jesus was the perfect substitute for man's sins. The Old Testament explains substitutionary death.[14] It is based on the transference principle in which the guiltiness of man was transferred to an innocent animal which then was slaughtered. When the animal died, according to this principle, the sins of the man which had been transferred to it died with it. Likewise, Jesus took upon Himself all the sins of the world and when He died all of man's sins died with Him. The substitutionary death of Jesus was prophesied by the ancient Hebrew prophets in the Old Testament. The most notable prophecy appears in Isaiah 53.

The New Testament contains many references to the substitutionary death of Christ. John the Baptist proclaimed that Jesus was a substitute for man's sins.[15] Jesus predicted His own death as a sin substitute.[16] In several passages the apostle Paul wrote that Jesus paid the price for the sins of the world.[17] The writer of Hebrews, the apostle Peter and the apostle John all wrote the same thing: Jesus Christ suffered the penalty for man's sins.[18]

When Christ took our place on that cross and in that tomb, He suffered our

death and hell.[19] The holy judgment of
God against sin fell on Him, resulting in
both physical death and spiritual separation
from God. But the story only begins with
the death of Christ.

No Remains

Let your mind flash back to Obi-wan
Kenobi as he dueled with Darth Vader. If
Darth had been struck by Kenobi's light
saber he would have died, for sure. But
Kenobi said if he himself were to die he
would only become more powerful!
Kenobi then offered himself as a sacrifice
in order to save those he loved.

Darth lashed out at Kenobi. But instead
of our seeing the mortally wounded
Kenobi, we see Darth incredulously prob-
ing through the pile of clothing on the
floor where Kenobi had slumped. There
was no body left to be found!

The mystery of Kenobi's disappearing
body was never explained in the movie.
But, in the real drama of Jesus Christ which
it illustrates so well, the Bible gives a clear
and wonderful explanation.

Victory Over Death

On the third morning following Christ's
crucifixion, Mary Magdalene and the other

Mary went to look at the tomb. But when they approached, they found the huge stone that had sealed the entrance to the tomb had been rolled away. Peering inside, they found the tomb completely empty, except for a pile of strips of linen that had covered the body of their Lord! Jesus had arisen!

Later, the Lord appeared to the two women, then to Cleopas, to the disciples and then to more than 500 people. You can read the entire account in all four Gospels—Matthew 28, Mark 16, Luke 24 and John 20.

Death could not keep Christ in the grave. Sin had no power over Him. Satan had been defeated.

Death has been swallowed up in victory.
Where, O death, is your victory?
Where, O death, is your sting?[20]

Just as Kenobi's sacrifice brought freedom to his people, the real substitutionary death of Jesus Christ and His resurrection have brought everlasting life and freedom from Satan, sin and death to those who believe in Him.

Kenobi remained in spirit with Luke Skywalker, speaking to his soul, giving wise counsel, leading and directing him onward. Well, I've got good news for you: Jesus Christ is alive today! He is seated at the right hand of God the Father in heaven, and, He is with us, too, in the person of His Holy Spirit. Those of us who believe in Christ and have repented of our sins and received Christ as our Lord and Savior, now have His Holy Spirit indwelling our lives: *forever!*

The same True Force—God Almighty—who created the universe and everything in it lives in the life of every believer through His Holy Spirit.

STAR WARS
Released by 20th Century-Fox

Princess Leia (Carrie Fisher), Chewbacca, Han Solo (Harrison Ford) and Luke Skywalker (Mark Hamill) discuss their best route of escape on the Death Star.

Chapter 9

The New Alliance

It would have been difficult to imagine that out of the Old Republic there would emerge the Alliance—a movement that started with only a small number of followers of the Force—because at that time, conditions in the Republic were worse than ever. The ways of the Force had all been forgotten, except by a devout few. And many of those never mentioned the name of the Force in public, for fear of reprisal by Imperial stormtroopers.

Most people accepted the harsh conditions under the New Order, somewhat begrudgingly, of course, but without much resistance. Many of them were reduced to poverty levels, eking out a meager existence and little else on barren, forsaken planets such as Tatooine. Luke's uncle Owen and aunt Beru, who had taken him in as an infant after his father's death, were typical.

But not far from the land homesteaded by Owen and Beru Lars, in land so barren that no kind of crop would grow, there lived Obi-wan Kenobi. Years ago he had gone into hiding to escape the purge of Jedi Knights by Darth Vader and the Imperial stormtroopers. Kenobi knew from the interplanetary grapevine that there were small systems scattered throughout the universe that resisted the oppressive tyranny of the Palpatine government. Banded together under the name "The Alliance," these people had set up a secret rebel base on the planet Alderaan.

But now, a new crisis. Alderaan was being threatened by an awesome new weapon being developed by Governor Tarkin called the Death Star, the planet destroyer.

Senator Leia Organa, a beautiful young girl who was secretly Princess Leia of the Alliance, knew the only chance they had to succeed in saving the Republic was to call upon the help of Obi-wan Kenobi. She trusted Obi-wan not only because of his distinguished military career in the Jedi Knights, but also because he, above anyone else, knew the ways of the Force best. And Obi-wan, after being contacted by Princess Leia, knew full well that the only chance the terribly outnumbered Alliance had was, indeed, to rely on the power of the Force.

So, along with his newfound companions, young Luke Skywalker, the skeptical Han Solo, Chewbacca and Threepio and Artoo, Kenobi set out on his mission to save the Republic from evil.

Kenobi was very encouraged when he finally reached the rebel stronghold. For there, gathered together from the far corners of the universe, were others who, like himself, were deeply committed to following the ways of the Force.

Strangers in the World

The people of the Alliance were destined to a new life, centered in the Force. They lived in the Galactic Empire, but they were never really a part of it.

In the real world, in the saga of mankind, we can see a clear parallel between the Alliance and the followers of Jesus Christ, the Church. Peter wrote, concerning the Church:

"You are a chosen people, a royal priesthood, a holy nation, a people belonging to God, that you may declare the praises of him who called you out of darkness into his wonderful light. Once you were not a people, but now you are the people of God; once you had not received mercy, but now you have received mercy. Dear friends, I urge you, as foreigners and strangers in the world, to abstain from sinful desires, which war against your soul. Live such good lives among the pagans that, though they accuse you of doing wrong, they may see your good deeds and glorify God on the day he visits us" (1 Peter 2:9-12).

What About the Jews?

But, wait a minute, you might ask, weren't the Jews the chosen people of God? That's right, but as the apostle Paul wrote to the Christians at Rome, God has given Israel a spirit of unbelief in Jesus Christ as the true Messiah: "What Israel sought so earnestly it did not obtain, but the elect did. The others were hardened, as it is written: 'God gave them a spirit of stupor, eyes so that they could not see and ears so that they could not hear, to this very day' " (Romans 11:7,8).

Here is a tremendous example of God's perfect trustworthiness. Even though the Jews refused to accept Jesus as their Messiah, God will stand by His promises to them, and in the end, all Israel will be saved! Paul quotes this tremendous promise of God, which was recorded by the prophet Isaiah: "The deliverer will come from Zion; he will turn godlessness away from Jacob. And this is my covenant with them when I take away their sins" (Romans 11:26,27). This carrying out of God's divine plan will take place at the very end of the age, when Jesus Christ returns.

The New Alliance

The Church is very much like the Alliance of *Star Wars.* It had a humble beginning, with only a few faithful followers at first. Just as the followers of the Force were set apart from the rest of the universe, so is the Church of Jesus Christ called out from the world.

The word "church" comes from a Greek term which, in the New Testament, refers to the body of believers in Christ who are "called out from the world" into Christian fellowship. It is the name used to identify either the whole Christian body, or the original group of disciples, or local groups of believers, or even the places in which they meet and worship.[1]

Members in the Church are usually considered to have three characteristics: They must be willing to repent of their sins, that is, to be sorry for committing them and then to detest them to the point of turning away from them; they must have received by faith Jesus Christ as their Savior and Lord; and they must be baptized as a public confession of that belief.[2]

The Church was founded on Peter's confession that Jesus is "the Christ, the Son of the living God" (Matthew 16:16). Jesus stated this when He answered, "And I tell you that you are Peter, and on this rock [that is, Peter's confession] I will build my church, and the gates of Hades will not overcome it" (Matthew 16:18). The Church's foundation is "the apostles and prophets, with Christ Jesus himself as the chief cornerstone. In him the whole building is joined together and rises to become a holy temple in the Lord" (Ephesians 2:20,21).

Though there are many assemblies of Christians throughout the world, they constitute a single body, indwelt by God's Holy Spirit.[3] The Church ministers to its individual members through its apostles, prophets, evangelists, pastors and teachers, in order "to prepare God's people for works of service, so that the body of Christ may be built up" (Ephesians 4:11,12). God calls from among His people bishops, deacons and elders to serve and care for the local churches.[4]

Through It All

Just as the religious remnant in *Star Wars* overcame evil through the power of the Force, so has the Church overcome Satan, sin and death through the power of Jesus Christ.

The Church has survived hostile religions, antagonistic governments, atheistic oppressors, lethargy from within and even apostasy, but through more than nineteen centuries, there has survived what at times has been only a small remnant of true followers of Christ. There will always be such a true following—at least, that is, until Christ returns for His Church as He promised on repeated occasions.

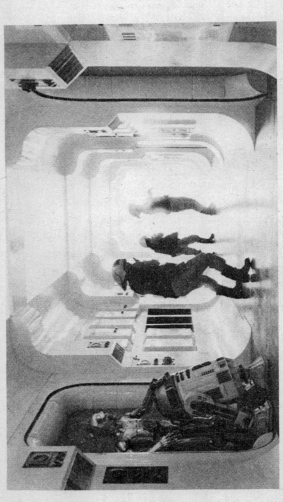

STAR WARS
Released by 20th Century-Fox

Artoo-Detoo and See-Threepio help-
lessly watch rebel troops defend the
Rebel Blockade Runner.

Chapter 10

The Daring Mission

Luke Skywalker and Obi-wan Kenobi blasted off into space with Han Solo aboard the pirate freighter, the *Millennium Falcon.* They were charted for lightspeed passage to the rebel outpost on the planet Alderaan at a far corner of the galactic heavens. But first they had to rescue Princess Leia from Governor Tarkin and Darth Vader on the Death Star.

A Supernatural Relationship

In many ways the Church is like that small band of religious zealots aboard the *Millennium Falcon.* Just as Obi-wan Kenobi gave them leadership, in the name of the Force, so did Jesus Christ, acting in the name and will of God the Father, serve— and continues to serve—as the head of His mystic body, the Church.[1] Even after Kenobi died for his disciples, he continued to function as their *spiritual* counselor, as evidenced by his supernatural return to give guidance to young Luke. While Christ died to save His Church from Satan's hold, He continues to love, nourish and cherish it.[2]

A Call to Heavenly Places

Like the remnant aboard the *Millennium Falcon*, the Church also has been called to heavenly places: "Since, then, you have been raised with Christ, set your hearts on things above, where Christ is seated at the right hand of God. Set your minds on things above, not on earthly things" (Colossians 3:1,2).

The Christian walk is truly a daring, out-of-this-world adventure! There are scary hazards, to be sure. Satan and his demons, the temptations to sin, and physical death, but Jesus holds authority and power over all these. Through His resurrection from the dead, He has given His believers victory over Satan, sin and death.

Even as Christians are out in the world, they do not conform to the world, but rather strive for holiness, patterning their lives after the perfect man, Jesus Christ.[3] Their primary calling is to praise and glorify Christ.[4]

The Great Commission

Next to worshiping Jesus Christ, the most important thing a Christian can do is to preach the good news of Christ, wherever he goes. It is an interesting parallel that while Obi-wan Kenobi returned in the spirit to give direction to young Luke, the Holy Spirit of God has been sent to indwell Christians, giving them untold comfort, understanding, wisdom, strength and power—and especially to be witnesses for Jesus Christ throughout the world.[5]

On another occasion, Christ gave to His Church what has become known as the Great Commission:

" 'All authority in heaven and on earth has been given to me. Therefore go and make disciples of all nations, baptizing them in the name of the Father and of the Son and of the Holy Spirit, and teaching them to obey everything I have commanded you. And surely I will be with you always, to the very end of the age' " (Matthew 28:18-20).

For more than nineteen centuries, Christ's Church has been carrying out this daring mission to reach the world with the gospel. Untold millions of believers have died the death of martyrs because of their faith and for helping to carry out the Great

Commission. Nations have gone to war over the fervent efforts of Christians to tell others about their beloved Lord Jesus Christ.

But none of this is surprising to believers, because Jesus said it would happen:

" 'If the world hates you, keep in mind that it hated me first. If you belonged to the world, it would love you as its own. As it is, you do not belong to the world, but I have chosen you out of the world. That is why the world hates you. Remember the words I spoke to you: "No servant is greater than his master." If they persecuted me, they will persecute you also. If they obeyed my teaching, they will obey yours also. They will treat you this way because of my name, for they do not know the one who sent me. If I had not come and spoken to them, they would not be guilty of sin. Now, however, they have no excuse for their sin. He who hates me hates my Father as well. If I had not done among them what no one else did, they would not be guilty of sin. But now they have seen these miracles, and yet they have hated both me and my Father. But this is to fulfill what is written in their Law: "They hated me without reason."

" 'When the Counselor comes, whom I

will send to you from the Father, the Spirit of truth who goes out from the Father, he will testify about me; but you also must testify, for you have been with me from the beginning' " (John 15:18-27).

Mission Accomplished

Jesus would not have sent His Church on this daring mission without giving them the power to accomplish it. This is one of the reasons for His sending the Holy Spirit. Even if believers are arrested and taken before atheistic courts, the Holy Spirit will be there with them, to give them the words of wisdom and testimony to say.

"On account of me," Jesus tells His Church, "you will stand before governors and kings as witnesses to them. And the gospel must first be preached to all nations. Whenever you are arrested and brought to trial, do not worry beforehand about what to say. Just say whatever is given you at the time, for it is not you speaking, but the Holy Spirit" (March 13:9-11).

Here, too, Jesus tells the Church that the mission of carrying the gospel to the world will be accomplished! Not long afterwards, the end of the age will come and Christ will return to planet earth—"and then the end will come," Jesus is quoted saying in Matthew 24:14.

More and more Christians are beginning to believe that the gospel could be preached to all nations in order to accomplish the Great Commission in this generation. They base their belief on the tremendous evangelistic movement on the part of the Church in many areas of the world. One organization in particular, Campus Crusade for Christ International working through local churches, recently mobilized and trained more than 300,000 Christian workers to reach some 200 major metropolitan areas of America and Canada with the gospel. And now, Campus Crusade is well along the way in carrying out a Great Commission strategy that will see the entire world reached by the Church with the gospel. The target date for accomplishing this mission: the end of 1980! Never before in history has there been such a thrust on the part of the Church to preach the good news about Jesus Christ.

Luke Skywalker and his fellow followers of the Force accomplished their daring mission to free Princess Leia and their countrymen from the bondage of the Imperial government. In like manner, the Church has been promised by Jesus Christ that it will succeed in preaching the gospel to all nations of the world—the good news that through His resurrection power He can save men from their sins and from spending eternity under the bondage of Satan.

STAR WARS
Released by 20th Century-Fox

Peter Cushing is Grand Moff Tarkin, Governor of the Imperial Outland regions and commander of the frighteningly powerful new battle station, the Death Star.

Chapter 11

The Demonic Duo

The Emperor Palpatine relied heavily on people of wicked character to help carry out his reign of terror against the people of the Force. His most effective assistants were Grand Moff Tarkin, governor of the Outland Regions, and Darth Vader, the Dark Lord of the Sith.

Governor Tarkin and Darth Vader possessed a brand of wickedness that bears sharp resemblance to a demonic duo the Bible tells us will appear in the end times, immediately in the years before Christ's second coming. These two infamous men of prophecy are best known as the Antichrist and the False Prophet.

As the two bases of the name "antichrist" indicate, this person will be against Jesus Christ. He and his sidekick, the False Prophet, will fill the world with wickedness as adversaries of Christ and His followers, and all Jews who will be looking for the coming of their Messiah.

Common Origins

Governor Tarkin rose up from the people of the Old Republic, which was without question the most powerful governmental force in all the known star system. Though many people in those early days followed the ways of the Force, Tarkin was an atheist in that he did not believe the Force was anything more than a myth.

The Antichrist of the Bible, in like manner, will rise to power through the government of the mightiest nation on the face of the earth.[1] He also will not be elected President of his country in the normal way (by popular vote), but will get into office as the result of a conspiracy, the nucleus of which will be ten politicians, industrialists and financiers.[2]

The prophet Daniel pictured the Antichrist as a monstrous king who, though of Jewish parentage, will be an atheist.[3] Daniel saw many characteristics of the Antichrist in the ancient enemy of the Jews, Antiochus Epiphanes: proud and arrogant, dealing in secrecy and deceiving people with ambiguous speech. A brilliant intellectual, he will possess both supernatural and political power.[4] The apostle John in the book of Revelation added another characteristic of the Antichrist—the fact that his name will be calculated to have the numerical value of 666.[5]

Just as Governor Tarkin called upon Darth Vader to use supernatural powers to accomplish his evil plans, the Bible tells us that Satan will give the Antichrist his "power and his throne and great authority," and that the False Prophet will perform many supernatural feats.[6]

Reign Over Babylon

The Governor's strategy called for gaining control over his outland district of the Republic, which was the most powerful district in all the Republic. From there, he would conquer the rebel base of the Alliance with his awful planet destroyer, the Death Star. And, after that? Who knows? Perhaps he would even attempt to overthrow the Emperor in an effort to take over the reigns of government of the entire Republic.

The treacherous way in which Tarkin betrayed a tentative peace agreement with Princess Leia only amplified the dark evil in his heart. He definitely was not a man to be trusted.

Satan's strategy for the Antichrist is strikingly similar. First, the Antichrist will become head of the mightiest nation on the face of the earth through a ten-man conspiracy of strong men in industry, commerce and finance. This nation is symbolically called "Mystery Babylon the Great" in the Bible. Once the most blessed by God of all nations, Babylon will quit using its wealth for God's purposes and instead use it for selfish gratification. In the end, Babylonians will turn away from God and actually worship Satan and his Antichrist!

The second phase of Satan's strategy calls for the Antichrist to gain control over the tiny nation of Israel. He will do this by signing a deceptive peace treaty in the Middle East which will allow him to introduce his "peace-keeping" troops into the region. But after three and a half years, he will break the peace treaty and expose his plan for world domination.[7]

Religious Persecution

Governor Tarkin was determined to wipe out every person in the galactic system who believed in what he called the "mythical" Force. Darth Vader, who well understood the power of the supernatural, was the governor's number one agent for stamping out the strong religious remnant. The galactic war was based on both political and religious issues, but no matter how much military might the Imperial government brought against the greatly outnumbered forces of the Alliance, it could not succeed in stamping them out. Tarkin's great hope lay in the success of the Death Star.

The Antichrist will carry out his vengeance against Christ by persecuting and killing His followers on earth during the last half of his seven-year reign.[8] And just as Darth Vader's supernatural powers were used by Tarkin, so will the False Prophet use his supernatural powers from Satan to assist the Antichrist in his quest for world political, economical and religious domination.[9]

Emperor Worship

The Antichrist's Middle East peace treaty will perhaps make it possible for Jews to rebuild their Holy Temple atop the Temple Mount in Jerusalem, where the Arab's Dome of the Rock Shrine now occupies some of the space. This Temple will be the location for the resumption of sacrifices and offerings, as these rites were discontinued after the Romans destroyed the second Temple in A.D. 70. But midway through his reign, the Antichrist will call a halt to the Temple sacrifices and offerings. He will set up his own throne in the Temple, calling himself God, and demanding that everyone worship him under the penalty of economic restrictions and even death.[10]

Things will begin to go awry in the kingdom of the Antichrist, however. Babylon's economy will falter, the martyrdom of Christ's followers will only be an inspiration and a witness to others to believe in and follow Christ, and several world powers will threaten his position in the Middle East. Much trouble will lie ahead for this man who-would-be-god.

STAR WARS

Released by 20th Century-Fox

Darth Vader and his Imperial guards take Princess Leia to the Death Star detention center.

Chapter 12

The Time of Chaos

In the years since Palpatine declared himself Emperor, the galactic system was shaken by war. There were harsh economic controls and widespread religious persecution. People like Luke's uncle Owen and aunt Beru were forced into a near-poverty existence. Bandits roamed the wilderness of planets like Tatooine, while Jawas were reduced to existing off junk and refuse. Racketeers gathered in dimly lit cantinas to plot their shady deals. Pirates and smugglers worked one end of the galaxy to the other.

The extermination of the Jedi Knights, who had had a stabilizing effect on society because of its religious fervor for the Force, ushered in this frightening time of lawlessness and immorality.

The End of the Age

The conditions found in the galactic system of *Star Wars* are much the same as those which we see in the world today, and which will only intensify as planet earth rushes toward the climax of history when this age comes to its end.

There is a name given to the last seven years of world history: "Daniel's Seventieth Week" (though it is commonly called the "Tribulation" period).

In the twenty-fourth chapter of the book of Matthew, some of the disciples of Jesus asked Him to explain the signs that will appear to indicate when the destruction of Jerusalem will occur, when the end of the age will come, and when He will return to establish His thousand-year reign on earth.

Signs of the Times

Jesus proceeded to characterize the Church age, citing conditions which would only intensify in the last seven years before His return. He said impostors would appear, claiming to be the returned Christ. False prophets will fill people's heads with lies. There will be wars and rumors of wars, famines and earthquakes throughout the world. People who believe in Him will be hated, betrayed, persecuted and even martyred. And many believers will engage in unspiritual behavior. The Antichrist ("abomination of desolation") will set up his throne in the rebuilt Jewish Temple in Jerusalem and proclaim to the world that he is god and is to be worshiped.

The apostle Paul repeated to the church at Thessalonica what must first take place before Christ returns:

"Concerning the coming of our Lord Jesus Christ and our being gathered to him, we ask you, brothers, not to become easily unsettled or alarmed by some prophecy, report or letter supposed to have come from us, saying that the day of the Lord has already come. Don't let anyone deceive you in any way, for that day will not come until the rebellion occurs and the man of lawlessness is revealed, the man doomed to destruction. He opposes and exalts himself over everything that is called God or is worshiped, and even sets himself up in God's temple, proclaiming himself to be God" (2 Thessalonians 2:1-4).

Daniel's Seventieth Week will begin when Satan's ambassador to earth, the Antichrist, signs a deceptive seven-year peace treaty with the nation of Israel. At the moment that treaty is signed, there will begin a seven-year countdown to the time of Jesus Christ's return to earth. When He returns, the present age will end and He will begin a fantastic new period of history on planet earth. Called the "Millennium," this will be one thousand years of peace under the rule of Christ over all the world.

World in Rebellion

But the seven years before Christ's return will be marked by a time of terrible lawlessness in the world. Now, the word "lawlessness" needs some explanation. When the law is mentioned, we usually think of man's laws—those which are written on a nation's lawbooks. But there is another kind of lawlessness: a complete disregard for God's laws. And man's laws and God's laws don't always correspond.

For example, our society today looks upon homosexuality as an alternative among consenting adults, the individual's right to which the law of the land should not interfere. But God's law, as spelled out in the Bible, clearly condemns homosexuality as a sin. Likewise, when a man and a woman live together outside of marriage, society and man's laws look upon this as an alternative life-style which individuals have a right to pursue without interference on the part of the law. But, again, God's law says otherwise: A couple who lives together outside of holy matrimony is committing the sin of adultery.

Prostitution is permitted in the state of Nevada, according to man's law. But God's law says prostitution is sinful adultery.

Adult bookstores and the pornography they peddle are legal according to man's laws in many cities. Yet God's law calls such activity licentiousness, which is sin. A publisher recently told a college class of journalism students, "If you want to become a successful publisher, start out by publishing pornography. There's a real need for professionally done pornographic books—most of what is on the market today is amateurishly done."

In New York City in 1975, there were more abortions than live births, according to a recent study. Those abortions were legal, in the view of man's laws, but they were illegal according to God's law which states, "Thou shalt not kill!"

In California, a couple can end their marriage by dissolution, without having to state any reasons. Again, man's law says this is legally the right of individuals to terminate a marriage. But God's law says to divorce one's mate, except on grounds of adultery, is sin.

Crime in Our Cities

But if man doesn't respect God's laws, why should he respect man's laws? Is it any wonder crime continues to increase in our nation's cities? How far will man's indifference to the laws of God and man go?

What happened in New York during the blackout of summer 1977? More than 3,000 people were arrested for looting and other crimes committed during the blackout. Looting alone reached near-riot proportions in parts of the city and the police had no way to cope with the mass demonstration of law-breaking. Only nine years earlier, when a blackout hit New York and much of the surrounding area, there were practically no reports of increased lawlessness! What is happening in America?

An ostrich-complex has taken hold of society: Bury your head in the sand and sin will go away! The courts are legalizing homosexuality, cohabitation, abortion and "quickie" divorces, thereby legitimatizing them in man's sight. These things are no longer wrong—no longer sin—in the eyes of man! But God's laws never change. These things are sin, no matter what man's courts of expedient law say they are. And the only power that will cause sin to go away is the forgiveness of God through His Son, Jesus Christ.

Well, listen, things are going to get much worse before they get better. All the lawlessness we see in our country today will seem like mere mischief compared to what tomorrow is going to bring. What's next? Get ready for it—*stringent economic controls, loss of more personal freedoms . . . and religious persecution!*

Religious Persecution Today

Many affiliate stations of the three major television networks refused to sell prime program time to a Christian organization during its evangelism campaigns in 1976. But in July 1977, on one of those same networks, Bill Moyer and his production team proceeded to air a special, during prime time, called "Born Again," which was highly critical of the evangelical movement in America today. Does the public no longer have access to television, *unless* the message meets the philosophical views of network executives?

What will be the result of lawlessness and religious persecution? Former Attorney General William Saxbe believes

America's soaring crime rate could push this nation into forming a national police force!

"As a society," Mr. Saxbe explained, "we seem to have absolutely lost our perception of a variety of things that can corrupt and distort the young. . . . Alcoholism has become perhaps our major health problem . . . pornography has become as widespread as baseball . . . the average eight-year-old has seen more violence on television than the average soldier encounters during a hitch in the Army.

"We should never doubt for a moment that there are men and forces at work in this country eagerly awaiting an opportunity to devise such a program as the first step toward total control over our lives. . . . National police can be used as an instrument of national repression—and they always wind up being run by somebody else. . . . Already we hear many say the answer to crime rests solely with more police, tougher police, more judges, more prosecutors, more prisons.

"If such a buildup should occur on a massive scale—beyond what may be reasonably needed—then we would see basic freedoms begin to dissipate. . . . Such a trend would be progressive. And if history teaches us anything, it is that freedoms willingly surrendered for any reason are never returned."

Immorality Leads to Lawlessness

Let us not forget that the cause of rebellion against man's laws stems from rebellion against God's laws. Billy Graham recently told the California State Legislature:

"Morals are sinking lower with every passing hour, and if they sink much lower ... we will head straight into the arms of a dictatorship in this country because America cannot survive without strong moral values."

Now, Dr. Graham isn't just guessing what the future is going to bring, he is restating what the Bible has to say about the end-times. Read what the apostle Paul wrote concerning morality in the end-times:

"But realize this, that in the last days difficult times will come. For men will be lovers of self, lovers of money, boastful, arrogant, revilers, disobedient to parents, ungrateful, unholy, unloving, irreconcilable, malicious gossips, without self-control, brutal, haters of good, treacherous, reckless, conceited, lovers of pleasure rather than lovers of God; holding to a form of godliness, although they have denied its power" (2 Timothy 3:1-5, *NASB*).

The Book of Destiny

The fifth chapter of the book of Revelation describes God's Book of Destiny for planet earth. Jesus Christ, the Lamb of God and Lion of Judea, is the only one worthy to open the seven seals of this book so that its contents might be revealed for mankind to consider.

Beginning in the sixth chapter, Jesus opens the seals, one at a time, revealing some insight into the terrible conditions of the time at the end of the age. The meaning of these seals are as follows:

First seal—*a rider on a white horse.* Though many suggestions have been offered as to the true interpretation of this symbol, it is likely that its true meaning lies in signifying man's vain attempts to bring peace to the world, and especially the peace hoped for and promised by the Antichrist in the end-times.

Second seal—*a rider on a red horse.* Man, because of his imperfections, when given the power to make peace, also corrupts that power and takes peace away. In the end-times, the Antichrist will first be known as a peacemaker, but then his image will change to warmonger.

Third seal—*a rider on a black horse.* Famines and plagues will intensify the world over during the end-times. Certainly, the harsh economic controls imposed by the Antichrist will only fan the flames of inflation and scarcities.

Fourth seal—*a rider on a pale horse.* Widespread death will result from famines and plagues and the Antichrist's artificially created food shortages, which result in mass starvation the world over.

Fifth seal—*martyrdom.* Keeping his threats as recorded in Revelation 13, the Antichrist will kill all who refuse to bear his mark (the number 666 or his name) and worship him. Christians and Messianic Jews will be the main target of his wrath.

Sixth seal—*disturbances in the heavens and on earth.* Earthquakes and a darkened sun characterize the upheaval in nature that will take place at the time of the very end, immediately before the return of Jesus Christ to earth.

Seventh seal—*the opened Book of Destiny.* The end of the age has come and God now reveals the destiny of the world through the symbolism of the sounding of seven trumpets and the pouring out of seven bowls of God's wrath.

The trumpets will bring about awful plagues that will affect one-third of the earth's land and water and living things, including all those who are not Christians or divinely protected Messianic Jews.[1]

The seven bowls of God's wrath comprise the judgment brought on by the sounding of the seventh and last trumpet. These are God's righteous judgments against the Antichrist, his spiritually and morally corrupt Babylonian empire, and all the people who choose to bear his mark.[2] But, as with the seven trumpet judgments, those who are Christians or divinely protected Jews will be spared these judgments. Christians will be spared on the basis that God's judgment against sin no longer applies to them because Christ paid that penalty already—nearly 2,000 years ago at Calvary.[3] The group of divinely protected Messianic Jews receive a special seal of protection from God, as explained in the seventh chapter of the book of Revelation.[4]

These terrible judgments of our righteous and just God will be poured out upon the earth at the end of the age, and are but a part of the many events which will take place at that time.

STAR WARS

Released by 20th Century-Fox

Luke Skywalker (Mark Hamill) is attacked by a Tusken Raider, a vicious desert bandit.

Chapter 13

The War of the Worlds

The Imperial troops for years had been rounding up rebels from their hideouts in worlds scattered throughout the galactic system. But in recent times there was renewed fervor among the religious Alliance to see the Republic restored to its former greatness. Grand Moff Tarkin, driven by his insatiable political ambitions to become emperor, was ruthless in his methods to quell the rapidly growing rebellion. And now, he was masterminding the final testing of the awesome and frightening planet destroyer, the Death Star. This insidious man-made planet was so large it could easily be mistaken from a distance as a small world.

Religious Fervor
The Alliance was surprisingly stronger

than Tarkin and Darth Vader had bargained for. The stepped-up persecution against these people, along with more frequent murders, by Imperial guards under Darth's command had only served to foster their greater reliance on the power of the Force.

This increasing religious fervor was spreading throughout the galactic system. Former followers of the Force were renewing their dedication to the ways of the Force. And there were many new converts, including Luke Skywalker and Han Solo.

Luke was only a small child when his father was murdered by the treacherous Darth Vader. As a Jedi Knight, his father had been a staunch believer in the Force. But Luke was too young at the time to learn the ways of the Force from his father. But now, thanks to Obi-wan Kenobi, Luke was one of many who were joining the Alliance and committing themselves to following the ways of the Force.

There were other new converts, like Han Solo, a Corellian, who had no religious background whatsoever. A skeptic at first, Solo finally was convinced to follow the ways of the Force—as evidenced when he said to Luke before the climactic battle of Yavin, "May the Force be with you!"

The Two Witnesses

Luke and Solo represented two distinct groups of believers: Luke, with his religious heritage, and Solo, who was from a totally nonreligious background.

The book of Revelation contains a prophecy of two similar groups of believers in the True Force. In the story of the two witnesses in the eleventh chapter, we read that these two witnesses are also two olive trees and two lampstands. This, of course, is figurative language. The answer to this riddle is found in other sections of the Bible.

In the first chapter of Revelation, we learn that lampstands are symbolic of Christ's universal Church. These two witnesses then are representatives of the true Church, yet, since they have different religious roots they are symbolized by two lampstands and not just one.

Furthermore, the eleventh chapter of the book of Romans gives the apostle Paul's analogy of two olive trees. He writes that a cultivated olive tree is symbolic of completed Jews—that is, Jews, who because of their belief in Jesus Christ, are Christians. Paul then states that the wild olive tree stands for Gentile (non-Jewish) people who believe in Christ. Yet, both groups are Christians and belong to Christ's Church.

In Luke and Solo, then, we see allegory for both Hebrew Christians and Gentile Christians. Just as these characters from *Star Wars* were oppressed by the Imperial forces of the Emperor, so will Hebrew Christians and Gentile Christians be persecuted by Satan's ambassador to planet earth, the Antichrist.

War Against Believers

The galactic war had seen many believers in the Force slain at the treacherous hands of Darth Vader and the Imperial stormtroopers. The Jedi Knights, deceived as they were, were all but obliterated. And now the shrewd and wicked mind of Governor Tarkin was planning to use the Death Star to completely wipe out the Force's people, by destroying their rebel stronghold on the fourth satellite of the planet Yavin.

This is an interesting parallel with Bible prophecy of the future. The Antichrist will attempt to do away with all believers in Christ as well as Messianic Jews in the region of Palestine, since this part of the world is said to be the religious center at that future time.

The two groups of witnesses in Revelation 11, we learn, are permitted to finish their 1,260-day campaign of aggressive evangelism in Palestine before the Antichrist begins to wage "war against them" and overcomes them and kills many of them, according to the *King James Version* of the bible.

This means that during the first half of Daniel's Seventieth Week (which is 1,260 days, or three and a half years), Christians will actively spread the good news about Christ around the world, without severe antichristian interference. But once the nations of the world have heard the gospel, then God will permit the Antichrist to set up his throne in the rebuilt Jewish Temple in Jerusalem and from there deal out his murderous vengeance upon all Christians for the remaining half of the "Tribulation" period (which is 42 months or 1,260 days long).[1]

Many Christians will be killed by the Antichrist in the last three and a half years of Daniel's Seventieth Week. Their bodies will not receive the dignity of burial, and those who follow the Antichrist will "gloat over them and will celebrate by sending each other gifts," because these witnesses had tormented them with their talk of

Jesus Christ and the impending judgment.[2]

The Last Battle

But all will not be going smoothly for the Antichrist and his wicked government. Other nations of the world, fearful of his ambition to become world dictator, begin to take action. The eleventh chapter of the book of Daniel prophesies how Russia and her satellite-countries (led by the "king of the North") will attack the Antichrist in his Middle East encampment. Surprisingly, the stronger forces of the Russians will be pushed back in a humiliating defeat.[3]

Next, the Antichrist will begin to hear rumors that an Oriental army of two hundred million troops is beginning to mobilize for an attack against him. By then, Russia will have prepared for another, stronger invasion of the Middle East. Even the confederated Arab states will prepare to battle the Antichrist. Thus, the stage will be set for the final battle of history—the battle of Armageddon![4]

The word Armageddon is derived from the valley of "Megiddo," where many of history's bloodiest battles have been fiercely fought. Located about ten miles south of Nazareth and fifteen miles inland from the Mediterranean, this was where

Gideon and his 300 mighty men won their victory over the Midianites.[5] It is where Saul and his sons battled against the Philistines and died.[6] And it is where King Josiah was killed by Egyptian invaders.[7]

Even after biblical times, many famous battles were fought at Megiddo. The Crusaders fought on this plain during the Middle Ages, followed by Napoleon and his army. And, as recently as 1918, the English general, Edmund H. Allenby, defeated the Turkish army there, thus beginning a chain of events which led to the reestablishment of the nation of Israel in 1948. But all of these historic battles fall into mere insignificance compared to the intensity and importance of the final battle of the ages that is to receive its name from this historic battlefield: the battle of Armageddon.

The battle of Armageddon is also called the battle of God Almighty.[8] This is because, while the armies of the Soviet bloc, the Orient and the Arab confederacy intend to attack the Antichrist, their objective suddenly changes completely. Instead, they are actually lured into attack position by Satan and the Antichrist and the False Prophet in an attempt to ward off a fantastic invasion from outer space, led by Jesus Christ.

The War Today

Though many Christians now alive may never face some of the things we have seen in the future, nonetheless, a spiritual battle continues to rage on and on, affecting virtually every person on the face of the earth.

The Bible gives a vivid description of Satan at war: "Your enemy the devil prowls around like a roaring lion looking for someone to devour. Resist him, standing firm in the faith, because you know that your brothers throughout the world are undergoing the same kind of sufferings" (1 Peter 5:8).

In *Star Wars* we saw a great deal of body armor which was used as protection during physical combat. Well, the Bible prescribes a coat of armor for the Christian as protection against *spiritual* attack by Satan and his demons:

"Put on the full armor of God so that you can take your stand against the devil's schemes. For our struggle is not against flesh and blood, but against the rulers, against the authorities, against the powers of this dark world and against the spiritual forces of evil in the heavenly realms. Therefore put on the full armor of God, so that when the day of evil comes, you may be able to stand your ground, and after you have done everything, to stand. Stand firm then, with the belt of truth buckled around your waist, with the breastplate of righteousness in place, and with your feet fitted with the gospel of peace as a firm footing. In addition to all this, take up the shield of faith, with which you can extinguish all the flaming arrows of the evil one. Take the helmet of salvation and the sword of the Spirit, which is the word of God. And pray in the Spirit on all occasions with all kinds of prayers and requests. With this in mind, be alert and always keep on praying for all the saints" (Ephesians 6:10-18).

Remember, though, that Christ has already defeated Satan, sin and death. Christians, too, have defeated these enemies, through Christ and through the witness of their life-changing, personal relationship with Him.[9]

Chapter 14

The Invasion from Outer Space

To young Luke Skywalker the Incom T-65 space fighter he was piloting was very similar to his skyhopper back on Tatooine. Though the instrumentation was necessarily simple, the tiny one-man, one-'droid ship was a complex innerspace weapons system. Its highly sophisticated firepower control computer could guide a space torpedo with pinpoint accuracy to all but the smallest of targets (as you no doubt know!).

As Luke looked outside his cockpit at the formation of fighters around him, he was surely struck with the awesome importance of the mission he was on. Failure would mean death for himself and many others, but success could be the beginning of the end for the oppressive Imperial government. It was a race against time: The

Death Star was orbiting into position for a clear blast at the Alliance's base on Yavin Four, and Luke and his compatriots were set on penetrating the Death Star's defense system to strike at its one vulnerable point that could bring about total destruction.

Somewhere in the thin atmosphere of the Death Star, Obi-wan Kenobi came to Luke in his fighter in spirit. His voice persuaded Luke to bypass the T-65's computerized fire-control system and permit the Force to give him perfect timing and coordination in releasing his deadly torpedos.

The Future Invasion of Planet Earth

This surprise attack holds many similarities to the planet earth's coming invasion from outer space. As explained in the Bible, the "invaders" will be none other than Jesus Christ and His believers returning in triumph! This glorious event, which the Church has anticipated for more than nineteen hundred years, is called the second coming of Christ. It is the primary event that will begin the period which the Bible calls the "day of the Lord."[1]

The second coming of Christ refers to the personal and visible return of Jesus with all of His followers from throughout history. It is one of the doctrinal corner-stones of the Christian faith. The language of Scripture is clear in that Jesus Christ is personally going to return! To the aston-ished, mourning, unbelieving world this wonderful event will show the unfailing truth of the Bible, God's Word.

The biblical references to Christ's re-turn are many. Jesus Himself tell of His second coming in John 14:3 and Matthew 24:29,30. The angels in Acts 1:11 pro-claimed He would return in the same manner in which He departed following His resurrection. Two of Christ's apostles, Peter and Paul, in their letters to the churches said that Jesus Christ was coming again (Philippians 3:20; 1 Thessalonians 4:15,16; Titus 2:13; 1 Peter 1:7,13; Hebrews 9:28).

The Time of the Invasion

Jesus was asked by His disciples when He would return. He answered by saying that He would return at the end of the time of great "tribulation," which is the end of Daniel's Seventieth Week:

" 'Immediately after the tribulation of those days the sun will be darkened, and the moon will not give its light, and the stars will fall from the sky, and the powers of the heavens will be shaken and then the sign of the Son of Man will appear in the sky, and then all the tribes of the earth will mourn, and they will see the Son of Man coming on the clouds of the sky with power and great glory' " (Matthew 24:29,30, *NASB*).

But when will Daniel's Seventieth Week end, so that Christ will return? Well, we know that this period is seven years in duration, and that it will start when the Antichrist signs a seven-year peace treaty with the nation of Israel. God has revealed this coming peace treaty to us (along with many other events) as a sign that the second coming is approaching.

The apostle Paul explains in the fifth chapter of 1 Thessalonians that there is no need for him to discuss the time of the second coming and the signs preceding it, because those who read the letter will understand this from previous information. In the fourth chapter earlier, Paul writes the same thing about brotherly love: "Now about brotherly love we do not need to write to you, for you yourselves have been taught by God to love each other."[2]

Now, some might say that this contradicts the statement of Jesus that "No one knows about that day or hour" when He will return.[3] But God's Word is without contradiction—there is a simple explanation.

Consider a woman who is pregnant. By determining the date of conception she knows *to expect* the birth of her baby in *approximately* nine months. Certainly, as she begins to notice the swelling of her stomach area and begins to feel the first movements of the baby within her, she has all the confirmation she needs to know that she is going to have a baby. But she won't know the exact day and hour.

The same is true with the second coming of Christ. From the time of the signing of the Israeli peace treaty, alert believers will know that Christ's return is approximately seven years away, *but* they will not know the exact day and hour. And you can be sure that there will be many certain signs along the way during the chaotic time of Daniel's Seventieth Week to confirm to believers that the return of Christ is ever so near.

One of those signs, as we have already discussed, will be that the good news of Jesus Christ will be preached throughout the world—and then the end will come, coinciding with Christ's return. Therefore, everyone will have the opportunity of hearing about Jesus Christ and can choose whether to follow Him or to bear the mark of allegiance to the Antichrist.

Other major signs of the second coming are the appearance of the Antichrist and wholesale lawlessness throughout the world,[4] an intensification of problems among nations and an increase of calamities in nature.[5]

A Spectacle in the Heavens

The second coming of Jesus Christ will be no secret to anyone. It will be a personal, visible sight of great splendor as He descends from heaven as a rider on a white horse in great power and glory, with His multitudes of saints.[6] And just in case a person is blind and can't *see* all of this happening, the archangel will announce Christ's coming with a loud shout. Here is the apostle Paul's description of the second coming:

"According to the Lord's own word, we tell you that we who are still alive, who are left till the coming of the Lord, will certainly not precede those who have fallen asleep. For the Lord himself will come down from heaven, with a loud command, with the voice of the archangel and with the trumpet call of God, and the dead in Christ will rise first. After that, we who are still alive and are left will be caught up with them in the clouds to meet the Lord in the air. And so we will be with the Lord forever" (1 Thessalonians 4:15-17).

Unfortunately, there will be many people who refuse to follow Christ and instead will worship the Antichrist.[7] To them, the second coming of Christ will catch them off guard, just as a thief catches someone sleeping unawares.[8]

Jesus, too, warns believers to be alert to the signs of His second coming, so that it will not catch them unawares. Immediately before the start of the battle of Armageddon, in fact, He gives this last warning: " 'Behold, I am coming like a thief. Blessed is the one who stays awake' " (Revelation 16:15, *NASB*).

The Purpose of the Invasion

Jesus Christ is coming back to planet earth to bring to a close a period of history which has been characterized by both rebellion against God and love of God. The specific purposes for His return are many. In the limited space here, however, we can only mention a few of the major ones:

To resurrect the dead in Christ. When a believer dies, life becomes separated from his physical body. But his spirit, which has been reunited with God's through the indwelling of the Holy Spirit at the time of belief, will not be separation from God—ever: This is the essence of eternal life. Now, the life which is separated from the body is the soul, and the soul of the believer immediately upon the death of the body, goes to be with Jesus Christ.

When Christ returns, He will resurrect the physical bodies of the dead in Christ and miraculously and completely transform them into supernatural or "glorified" new bodies, like His. The promise of this resurrection is to be found in 1 Thessalonians 4:13-16, and the promise of new glorified bodies can be located in 1 Corinthians 15:51-54.[9]

To gather together all living saints. At the time of Christ's return, there will be surviving believers—some who have not been killed at the hands of the Antichrist, or died some other kind of death. There is a tremendous promise in the Bible for these surviving saints. Christ will return to first resurrect the dead in Christ, then, "We who are still alive and are left will be caught up with them in the clouds to meet the Lord in the air. And so we will be with the Lord forever" (1 Thessalonians 4:17).[10]

And, just like the dead in Christ, the

survivors who are caught up will also receive new, glorified bodies!

To reveal Himself and His resurrected and gathered saints, to be glorified in them. When Jesus Christ is viewed by the world at the time of His second coming, He will have with Him all the resurrected saints from ages past, as well as the surviving believers of Daniel's Seventieth Week, who will have just been gathered from throughout the world.

In highly poetic language, the return of Christ with His saints is described in the book of Revelation:

"I saw heaven standing open and there before me was a white horse, whose rider is called Faithful and True. With justice he judges and makes war. His eyes are like blazing fire, and on his head are many crowns. He has a name written on him that no one but he himself knows. He is dressed in a robe dipped in blood, and his name is the Word of God. The armies of heaven were following him, riding on white horses and dressed in fine linen, white and clean. Out of his mouth comes a sharp sword with which to strike down the nations. He will rule them with a rod of iron. He treads the winepress of the fury of the wrath of God Almighty. On his robe and on his thigh he has this name written: King of kings and Lord of Lords" (Revelation 19:11-16).[11]

To win the battle of Armageddon and judge the nations. If you think the light sabers of *Star Wars* were deadly weapons, Jesus Christ has an even deadlier sword! In the book of Revelation He is seen winning the battle of Armageddon, using a sharp sword with which to strike down all the ungodly nations of the world. But since the sword is described as coming out of His mouth, it probably isn't a real sword at all, but simply a figurative way of showing that Christ need only *speak* the command and all the world's nations will be punished for their sins.[12]

Just as the Death Star came to sudden destruction, so will the kingdom of the Antichrist—Babylon the Great.[13]

To judge the Antichrist and his followers. The Death Star came to its end in a ball of fire. With it was consumed the wicked Grand Moff Tarkin, whom we earlier discussed as being the counterpart of the Antichrist. Well, Christ has a special lake of burning fire reserved especially for the Antichrist and his followers, for eternity.

The apostle Paul writes that the Lord Jesus will overthrow the Antichrist "with the breath of His mouth" and destroy him by "the splendor of his coming" (2 Thessalonians 2:8).

This passage refers to the *physical* death of the Antichrist, while his *spiritual* death is his banishment forever in the lake of burning fire:

"But the beast (Antichrist) was captured, and with him the false prophet who had performed the miraculous signs on his behalf. . . . The two of them were thrown alive into the fiery lake of burning sulfur" (Revelation 19:20).

To establish His kingdom. Following the destruction of the Death Star, we find our heroes zooming off into space aboard the space freighter, *Millennium Falcon.* The word "millennium" is actually a technical Bible term which refers to the thousand-year reign of Christ on earth, following His second coming. During this time, He will set up His kingdom and rule with His saints in perfect peace and harmony.[14]

To save the remnant of Israel. The true remnant of Israel, a group of 144,000 Messianic Jews, according to Revelation 8, will miss the gathering of believers at Christ's return, but they will see Him when He returns and immediately recognize Him as their Messiah, and bow down to worship

Him. Since they will have earlier received a special seal of protection against God's destroying wrath in the end-times, they will go on into the Millennium to populate it.[15]

To bind Satan. During Christ's millennial reign, Satan will be bound, only to be released for a short time at the end of the thousand years. At that time, he will make one more vain attempt at leading the nations away from Christ, but he will be captured quickly and cast into the lake of burning fire where he will spend eternity in torment with the Antichrist, the False Prophet and all those who refused to receive Christ as Savior and Lord.[16]

To bless creation. Once again there will be harmony within the universe:

"The creation waits in eager expectation for the sons of God to be revealed. For the creation was subjected to frustration, not by its own choice, but by the will of the one who subjected it, in hope that the creation itself will be liberated from its bondage to decay and brought into the glorious freedom of the children of God. We know that the whole creation has been groaning as in the pains of childbirth right up to the present time" (Romans 8:19-22).

To reward His believers. All believers in Christ are assured of eternal salvation with

Christ. But now, just as Luke and Solo received rewards for their deeds, believers will receive rewards from Christ for theirs: "For the Son of Man is going to come in his Father's glory with his angels, and then he will reward each person according to what he has done" (Matthew 16:27).[17]

The invasion of planet earth by Jesus Christ and His believers will bring history around full circle. All people who choose to receive Christ as their Savior and Lord will enjoy everlasting fellowship with Him. Sin and death will be no more, and Satan and his followers will spend eternity totally separated from God.

Chapter 15

The Voyage to Eternity

Luke Skywalker *knew* that he had been destined for something beyond the day-to-day monotony and meaningless existence on the dusty, scorching hot plains of Tatooine. Ever since he could remember he had wanted to do something that mattered, something with purpose, something significant. He would gaze into the sky above Tatooine at the myriad star systems beyond, and somehow sense that he belonged in another world. The stars seemed to beckon him somewhere else.

But it was Obi-wan Kenobi who unlocked the mysteries of life for young Luke. For Obi-wan introduced Luke to the Force, and impressed upon him that to follow the ways of the Force was to realize life's fullest purpose and meaning.

The Call of Destiny

But what about you? What are you doing with your life? Do you have any meaningful purpose? What really matters in life? What are you living for? Where are you going? Like young Luke Skywalker, do you feel a voice whispering to you, urging you on to some greater destiny? That is the voice of the Spirit of God. How long have you ignored it? Well, don't turn away from Him any longer.

Now, I don't know what your understanding of God is, but the Bible says He goes beyond being a mere concept, or a philosophy, or even an impersonal force. He is more, much more. He is a Spirit Being with personality. He created the world, the universe and everything in it, including you. He didn't make you and the rest of creation to go spinning, uncontrolled, through the depths of darkness in outer space. No, He created you and all things with a purpose.

Let me paraphrase for you the wonderful verse from 1 Peter 2:9: "You are a chosen person, a royal priest, a citizen of a holy nation, a person belonging to God, that you may declare the praises of Him who called you out of darkness into His wonderful light."

As incredible as it might seem, God loves you and has a wonderful plan for your life. He wants you to be His child—a child of God!

How can it be done? Humanly speaking, it can't! But God has provided you with a special vehicle. Let's call it the *Starship Faith.* Jesus Christ invites you to come aboard and by faith become a child of God and journey into eternity. For it's impossible to take this voyage without faith. This doesn't mean that you must know how to pilot a starship. It doesn't mean you must know how to chart the route among the stars and the planets. Nor does it mean that you must have a great deal of knowledge about God, the Bible or eternity. You don't need to understand complex theology at all. You only need to place your simple faith, or trust, in the person of Jesus Christ and rely on His promises as found in the Bible. That's all that's required for you to get from here to eternity.

Spiritual Laws

When an orbiting satellite loses velocity, it begins a slow descent back to earth that will end in a fast and fiery reentry into the atmosphere. There are no other alternatives—this is determined by the law of gravity. And gravity is only one of many physical laws which govern the physical universe.

There are also spiritual laws which govern your relationship with God. The Bible explains these laws. The first one which you should know is that God loves you and offers a wonderful plan for your life.

The proof of God's love for you is found in His Son, Jesus Christ, as revealed in the Bible:

"For God so loved the world that he gave his one and only Son, that whoever believes in him shall not perish but have everlasting life. For God did not send his Son into the world to condemn the world, but to save the world through him. Whoever believes in him is not condemned, but whoever does not believe stands condemned already because he has not believed in the name of God's one and only Son" (John 3:16-18).

God's plan for your life has a twofold application. As we have just read, He offers everlasting life to all who believe in His Son. But He also offers a life full of meaning and purpose while we are on the planet earth. Jesus Christ promised, "I have

come that they may have life, and have it
to the full" (John 10:10).

Lost in Darkness

Many people are not living a full and
meaningful life with Christ because they
are lost in the vast darkness of spiritual
space called sin. They are the children of
darkness, separated from the light of God
by sin. Actually, the Bible says, "All have
sinned and fall short of the glory of God"
(Romans 3:23), and that "the wages [pay-
ment] of sin is death [spiritual separation
from God]" (Romans 6:23).

Without God, man is wandering aim-
lessly through the sinful darkness of his
existence, trying to find God and a full and
meaningful life through his own efforts,
such as a moral life, philosophy or religion.
But none of these can bring a person from
the darkness into the light.

Into the Light

The only way a person can find his way
out of the sinful darkness is through Jesus
Christ. Only through Him can you know
and experience God's love and plan for
your life.

"This is the message we have heard
from him and declare to you: God is light;

in him there is no darkness at all. . . . But if we walk in the light, as he is in the light, we have fellowship with one another, and the blood of Jesus [which he shed for us on the cross], purifies us from every sin" (1 John 1:5-7).

God proved His love for you when He sent His Son to die in your place: "But God demonstrates his own love for us in this: While we were still sinners, Christ died for us" (Romans 5:8).

Jesus said, "I am the light of the world. Whoever follows me will never walk in darkness, but will have the light of life" (John 8:12).

Born Again

At the time a person becomes a true Christian, he receives God's free gift of eternal life. That person becomes alive spiritually, where before he was dead. In this sense, he becomes spiritually "born again."[1]

But since eternal life is a gift, it must be received. You must *receive* Jesus Christ as Savior and Lord, then you can know and experience God's love and plan for your life: "Yet to all who received him, to those who believed in his name, he gave the right to become children of God" (John 1:12).

Now, let me remind you, we are traveling aboard our imaginary starship called *Faith* in our journey into eternity. Faith is the only way in which you can receive Christ and His promise of eternal life: "For it is by grace you have been saved, through faith—and this not from yourselves, it is the gift of God—not by works, so that no one can boast" (Ephesians 2:8,9).

Come Aboard

Jesus Christ is inviting you to come aboard the *Starship Faith*—to place your trust in Him, and follow Him on the most thrilling adventure known to man. The call of destiny—the small voice you have heard for so long in your mind and heart is that of Jesus Christ. He's knocking at the door of your heart right now, asking you to invite Him in: "Behold," He says, "I stand at the door and knock; if any one hears My voice and opens the door, I will come in to him" (Revelation 3:20, *NASB*).

Remember, now, as you board the *Starship Faith*, you are traveling from the darkness into light. Therefore all things that belong to the darkness must be left behind. You must turn away from the sinful past and look to the future in Christ.

God knows what is going on in your

head and heart at this very moment. Though He is more concerned with the attitude of your heart than the words of your mouth, it might be helpful for you to express the desire of your heart by saying the following suggested prayer:

"Lord Jesus, I need your love and direction in my life. I need you as my Savior. Thank You for dying on the cross for my sins. I open the door of my life and receive You as my Savior and Lord. Thank You for forgiving my sins and giving me eternal life. Take control of my life and make me the kind of person You want me to be. Amen."

If you prayed that prayer with all sincerity, you can know that Christ is in your life, that you are a child of God, that your sins are forgiven and that you have eternal life! You can believe these things because they are promised by God in His Word, the Bible. Jesus promised He would come into your life if you opened the door to your heart (Revelation 3:20). He promised, too, that He would give you the gift of eternal life:

"God has given us eternal life, and this life is in his Son. He who has the Son has life; he who does not have the Son of God does not have life. I write these things to you who believe in the name of the Son of God so that you may know that you have eternal life" (1 John 5:11-13).

Now it is important for you to remember that the promise of God's Word, the Bible—*and not your feelings*—is your authority for knowing that you are a Christian.

"But you are a chosen people, a royal priesthood, a holy nation, a people belonging to God, that you may declare the praises of him who called you out of darkness into his wonderful light. Once you were not a people, but now you are the people of God; once you had not received mercy, but now you have received mercy.

"Dear friends, I urge you, as foreigners and strangers in the world, to abstain from sinful desires, which war against your soul. Live such good lives among the pagans that, though they accuse you of doing wrong, they may see your good deeds and glorify God on the day he visits us" (1 Peter 2:9-12).

Congratulations on coming aboard the *Starship Faith*. You have just begun the most fantastic adventure a person could ever experience! A full and meaningful life in Christ.

May the True Force be with you, always and forever!

RESPONSE PAGE

(If you have just received Jesus Christ as your Savior and Lord and would like more information on how to experience the abundant Christian life, or if you would like more information on how to become a Christian, fill out this form and mail it today.)

_____ Please send me more information on how I can become a Christian.

_____ I have just received Jesus Christ as my Savior and Lord and would appreciate more information on how to experience the abundant Christian life.

_____ Please inform me of other materials for Christian growth.

Name _____

Address _____

City _____

State _____ Zip _____

Address all correspondence to the author:
Frank Allnutt
P.O. Box 5049
Blue Jay, CA 92317

FOOTNOTES

Chapter 2

1. Francis A. Schaeffer, *How Should We Then Live?* Old Tappan, NJ: Fleming Revell, 1976. (Author's written permission to use has been requested).
2. Ibid., p. ____.
3. Bill Bright, *A Movement of Miracles.* Arrowhead Springs, CA: Campus Crusade for Christ, Inc., 1977.

Chapter 3

1. Genesis 22:8,14
2. Exodus 17:15
3. Judges 6:24
4. John 14:27
5. Jeremiah 23:6
6. Ezekiel 48:35
7. Matthew 28:20
8. Psalm 46:7,11
9. e.g., Isaiah 17:6; Zephaniah 2:9

10. Isaiah 1:24
11. 1 Samuel 15:29
12. Daniel 7:9,13,22
13. Hebrews 13:8
14. Exodus 3:14
15. Isaiah 46:9,10
16. Exodus 20

Chapter 4

1. Revelation 12:4
2. Matthew 25:41
3. Genesis 2;3
4. 1 John 3:10
5. Genesis 1:28
6. 1 John 5:19
7. John 14:30
8. Revelation 9:11; 12:10; 1 Peter 5:8; 2 Corinthians 6:15; Matthew 9:34; 12:24; 2 Corinthians 4:4; John 8:44; Ephesians 2:2; Revelation 20:2

Chapter 5

1. Job 38:7
2. Job 5:1; Psalm 89:5,7; Daniel 8:13
3. Job 4:18; Matthew 25:41; 2 Peter 2:4; Revelation 12:9
4. 1 Kings 19:5-7
5. 2 Kings 19:35

6. 2 Samuel 24:16
7. Genesis 32:1; Joshua 5:13-15
8. 1 Kings 22:19-22; 2 Kings 6:17
9. Daniel 8:16; 9:21; Luke 1:19,26
10. Daniel 10:13,21; 12:1; Jude 9; Revelation 12:7
11. Isaiah 6:1-3; Ezekiel 10:14
12. Mark 3:22
13. Luke 11:14; Mark 9:17; Luke 8:27
14. Revelation 16:13,14
15. Matthew 12:28
16. Luke 9:1; 10:17
17. Mark 9:38

Chapter 6

1. Revelation 22:16
2. See also John 6:42,51; 7:29; 8:23, 42,59; Exodus 3:13,14; John 17:24
3. John 1:1-3
4. Genesis 3:15
5. Deuteronomy 18:18,19
6. Psalm 2:2,6,7,12
7. Isaiah 9:6,7; 53:4-12
8. Micah 5:2

Chapter 7

1. John 13:2

Chapter 8

1. Galatians 3:13; 4:4,5
2. Hebrews 2:14,15
3. Matthew 26:28; Hebrews 9:14-16
4. Hebrews 9:26-28; 10:12
5. Romans 8:2-4
6. 1 John 4:9-11; Romans 5:8
7. Isaiah 53:4-6,8,10; Matthew 26:39; Hebrews 10:9,10
8. Romans 3:25,26
9. Ephesians 5:25-27; Acts 20:28
10. 2 Corinthians 5:18-20
11. Romans 5:12; 6:23
12. See also John 3:1-5
13. John 8:29; 14:30; 2 Corinthians 5:21; 1 Peter 2:22; 1 John 3:5; Hebrews 4:15; 7:26
14. Leviticus 1:4
15. John 1:29
16. Matthew 26:28
17. Romans 4:25; 1 Corinthians 15:3; 2 Corinthians 5:21; Galatians 1:4
18. 1 Peter 2:24; 3:18,19; 1 John 4:10
19. Matthew 27:46,50
20. 1 Corinthians 15:54,55

Chapter 9

1. Ephesians 5:27; Acts 2:47; Romans

16:5; 1 Corinthians 11:18; 14:19,28. See also 1 Corinthians 12:18 and Acts 8:1.
2. Matthew 16:16-18; Acts 2:38-41
3. 1 Corinthians 12:12,13; John 14:17; Acts 2:4
4. Acts 6:2-6; 14:23; 1 Timothy 3

Chapter 10

1. Colossians 1:18; Ephesians 1:22; 5:24
2. Acts 20:28; Ephesians 5:23-29. See also 1 Corinthians 6:11
3. Ephesians 1:4; 2:21; 4:13; 5:27
4. Ephesians 1:6; 3:21
5. John 14:26; Acts 1:8

Chapter 11

1. Revelation 13:1; 17:3,9-13
2. Daniel 11:21; Revelation 17:12,13. See also Daniel 8:8,11; 1 Peter 5:13; Revelation 13:1-3; 17;18
3. Daniel 11:36,37
4. Daniel 8:23-25
5. Revelation 13:18
6. Revelation 13. See also 17:8,11,13,17; 2 Thessalonians 2:6-8
7. Jeremiah 50; 51; Daniel 9:27; Revelation 17

8. Daniel 8:25; Revelation 11:7; 13:7,10, 15; 17:14
9. Revelation 13:13-18
10. Daniel 9:27; 2 Thessalonians 2:4

Chapter 12

1. Revelation 8:6-9; 21; 11:15-19
2. Revelation 16
3. Romans 8:1
4. Note: The second multitude mentioned in this chapter are Christians in heaven, right after the return of Christ.

Chapter 13

1. Matthew 24:14-22; 2 Thessalonians 2:4; Revelation 13:5-10; 2 Thessalonians 2:6-8
2. Revelation 11:7-10. (Note: The Greek term for "days" in vv. 9 and 11 should properly be translated "years"; Luke 1:7,18
3. See also Ezekiel 38:14-17 and Joel 2:1-10,20
4. Revelation 9:13-16
5. Judges 7
6. 1 Samuel 31
7. 2 Kings 23. See also the victory of Deborah and Barak over the Canaanites

(Judges 4;5) and the death of Ahaziah
by Jehu (2 Kings 9:27)
8. Revelation 16:14
9. Revelation 12:11

Chapter 14

1. 2 Thessalonians 2:1-3
2. 1 Thessalonians 4:9
3. Matthew 24:36
4. 2 Thessalonians 2:3
5. Matthew 24:1-35
6. Jude 14; Zechariah 14:5; Matthew
   16:27; 24:26,27; 25:31; Acts 1:9,11;
   Colossians 3:4; 1 Thessalonians 3:13;
   Revelation 1:7; 19:11-16
7. Revelation 13:4
8. Matthew 24:42,43; Luke 21:34,36; 1
   Thessalonians 5:2,3; 2 Peter 3:10;
   Revelation 3:2,3
9. See also Ephesians 2:1-3; Philippians
   3:20,21
10. See also Matthew 24:31; 2 Thessa-
    lonians 2:1-3
11. See also Colossians 3:4; Zechariah
    14:5; 1 Thessalonians 3:13; 2 Thessa-
    lonians 1:10
12. Revelation 19:15,19-21; Matthew
    25:31,32; Joel 3:1,2,12; 2 Thessa-
    lonians 1:7-9; Isaiah 24:21-23

13. See Revelation 16:17-21; 18; 19:11-21; Ezekiel 38:17-22; 39:1-6; Zechariah 13:8,9; Jeremiah 23:3-6

14. Revelation 11:15; 20:4; Daniel 7:13,14; Luke 21:27,31; 2 Timothy 4:1; Zechariah 14:9; Matthew 25:31; Micah 4:3,4; Isaiah 2:4

15. Revelation 8; Acts 15:16; Zechariah 14:3,4; Joel 3:15,16

16. Revelation 20:1,2

17. See also 1 Corinthians 4:5; 2 Timothy 4:8; 1 Peter 5:4

Chapter 15

1. Read John 3:18.

Allegorical cast of characters from
STAR WARS

STAR WARS	THE BIBLE
The Force	God
Obi-wan Kenobi	Jesus Christ/Holy Spirit
Luke Skywalker	Hebrew Christians
Han Solo	Gentile Christians
Princess Leia Organa and the Alliance	Israel/the Israeli Remnant in the End-Times/The Church
Kenobi's Disciples	Christ's Disciples
Emperor Palpatine	Satan
Grand Moff Tarkin	Antichrist
Darth Vader	False Prophet/Judas Iscariot
Imperial guards & stormtroopers	Demons and Evil Spirits/Non-Christians

Other books by Frank Allnutt:
The Peacemaker
Antichrist: After the Omen
Kissinger: Man of Destiny
With Josef Korbel:
In My Enemy's Camp

ABOUT THE AUTHOR

Frank Allnutt is well qualified to write this book. Having earned his B.A. degree in Radio-Television-Film from Denver University, he received his early training in the publicity department at the Walt Disney Studios and went on to become public relations manager of the Disney master planning and design corporation. He has written several Christian books and numerous magazine articles and hosted a weekly program on a Los Angeles Christian TV station. The inspirational story of how he became a Christian in 1971 has appeared in several Christian magazines, including Billy Graham's *Decision*. Since his conversion, he has served as a marketing and mass communications consultant to a number of Christian organizations. He lives with his wife and three children in the mountain resort of Lake Arrowhead, east of Los Angeles.